Fables
by jambbal

simple stories for complex people...and children

NSC Publishing
New York

Fables

by jambbal

simple stories for complex people…and children

copyright © 2009 *jambbal*

All Rights Reserved

No part of this book may be used or reproduced in any manner whatsoever without the written consent of the author, except in the case of brief quotations embodied in critical articles and reviews or "*jambbal's* messages".

Except for the photograph at the end, any resemblance in this collection to a person, animal or plant, living or dead, is purely coincidental.

Published by NGC Publishing
New York

To submit comments, contact:
fablesbyjambbal@nycap.rr.com

To order copies of this book, go to:
fablesbyjambbal.com

Printed by RJ Communications
on recycled, acid-free paper
www.rjcom.com

ISBN: 978-0-578-01073-1

dedicated to Mary Kay,
the source of my inspiration,
the destination of my eternal love

Fables

by jambbal

simple stories for complex people...and children

Fables by jambbal

Table of Contents

Foreward by an African Lungfish	7
Introduction to *jambbal*	11
The Bee and the Forest Dwellers	13
The Snail with a Broken Shell	15
The Antarctic Bird Who Couldn't Fly	19
The Finicky Frog	23
The Scared Stream	25
The Divot	29
The Caterpillar and the Fawn	33
The Man of the Forest	37
The Jealous Herd of Jerseys	41
The Bear and the Beehive	45
The Beaver and the Otter Gang	49
The Hammerhead and the Humpback	53
The Tree Elder	57
The Boding Bacteria	61
The Wisdom of the Wapiti Cow	65
The Holy Dale	67
The Vixen and the Grouse	71
The Peacock and the Blue Jay	73
The Terrier and the Tiger	75
The Wayward Wolf	77
The Oak Tree and the Squirrels	81
The Adopted Squirrel	83
The Weather Forecasters	87
The Bull and the Bear	91
The Bald Eagle and the Golden Eagle	95
The Wandering Albatross	97
The Lamb, the Ram and the Ewe	101
Lady Springbok and Mama Cheetah	105
The Song of the Swan	107
The Source	109

Foreword
by an African Lungfish

For reasons beyond my understanding, the fabulist you know as *jambbal* approached me last January and asked that I write a foreword for his book of fables. I had not met him before and have not since that initial meeting followed by a second, which is when I dictated these words to him. Since I have no grasping fingers, I don't write myself, which this fellow already seemed to know when he issued his invitation, his pen and pad in hand.

This *jambbal* fellow seemed sincere and genuinely dedicated to his fables project, so I decided to consider his request. After all, he did wait patiently for more than a few years to come to my residence to meet me. He had to wait for the drought to be ended by a substantial rainy season. That's when I revived from my dormant state to surface, move again, breathe openly instead of through the dry mud and, of course, have a proper meal and create more lungfish.

He was there on the edge of the riverbed, in the rain, on his haunches, waiting for me to reappear from my long estivation. As I broke through my protective encasement and poked my head up, he greeted me as if he knew me and was anticipating my reappearance above ground.

"Welcome back, Lungfish," he said. "I arrived a few days ago waiting for you. I'd like you to consider helping me with a project, if you will." He then began reciting his fables to me. As I listened, I must say they are well written and I understood most of the material, but I also have a warning for you, the reader, as you will see shortly.

When he finished, he simply waited quietly for me to respond. I know about waiting quietly, perhaps more than most species; it is in my nature. His calm assured me of his appreciation of my nature. I asked him: "Why would you want me to contribute to your project?"

He replied directly as though he had been anticipating my question for all the years he had been waiting for the opportunity to have me ask it. "There are two reasons I have chosen you. First, in our world of speed and brevity and change, you represent a species from 400 million years ago; therefore, you bring to all species the qualities of calmness, longevity and stability. Our world needs those qualities more than ever."

He continued: "Second, you represent the secret of how a species can adapt from one environment to a completely different environment. Your ancestors discovered how to move from water to land, how to breathe air through lungs instead of gills, and how to find food out of the water instead of just in it. In the coming centuries for all species, we may find ourselves in dire need of radically changing our environment to survive, perhaps even on another planet as we deplete the resources of this one. Your lessons of survival are still relevant to all of us even millions of years later. I thank you for that."

His words made sense to me, his purpose even more. Yet, being a creature of deliberation and gradual progress, I told him I would consider his request, if that were acceptable, and invited his return toward the end of the rainy season before I submerged back into my protective dry mud shell. He smiled and agreed.

Upon his return a few months later, I dictated these words you now read. Even though I do not offer complete endorsement of this project, as explained below, I thought it sufficiently worthy of my contribution and, if he accepted it, my cautionary remarks. He did accept my contribution, word for word without edit, corroborating one of the reasons I decided to do it: his acceptance of the world and all its inhabitants as they are.

This *jambbal* person strives to make life better, but goes about it respectfully, not invasively or with arrogance. My species, indeed most species, don't even have a word for arrogance. Most of us know what we know and what we don't know, so we simply call it ignorance when we don't know something. Humans devalue ignorance, so they try to mask it with the pretense of knowledge. Then, because that pretense causes a lot of trouble, it's once again devalued by calling it arrogance. I imagine it must be very difficult to learn when one has a confusing map like that.

Speaking of maps, no species other than humans draw maps. What I mean is that we don't carve up the planet with lines and names like you do. We mark territories for such reasons as finding food, seeking shelter, raising our young, and then we defend that space, if necessary. For example, I live in a space you call Africa. You call me an African Lungfish. Well, that sounds so strange to me that I'd laugh, if I could. I know who and what I am and who and what I'm not. You may need to name me so you think you know me, but I am not in need of a name.

Now for these fables. The man you call *jambbal* tries to draw lessons for the benefit of your species from the rest of us. The analogies he draws may be useful to you, but I caution you to read the fables with an understanding that our species are quite different from you and from one another. We may share many characteristics, but our fates may not be the same much less the paths we take to get to them. His lessons may not apply.

One of the limitations you may confront in reading these tales is your sense of superiority over the rest of us. Humans have historically used us for their own benefit in many ways, including but not limited to food, labor you don't want to or can't perform, especially hard labor, transportation, warning systems, experiments on how life works, adornment of your bodies, entertainment for your minds, competition and companionship. As you often say yourselves, "It's all about you!"

Superiority serves well in the hunt for food, for territory, for mates, for survival; it ill serves in the hunt for knowledge. The intellectually superior seek not what they already believe themselves to know, thus aborting any quest for that knowledge. Like arrogance, intellectual superiority is borne of absence, not plenty. Any non-human attempting to survive with arrogance or intellectual superiority soon perishes in accordance with the forces of nature. Humans would do well to consider that consequence.

The ultimate act of irony is your species' belief that you can study your brain with your own brains. Some day you may discover the study of the brain by the brain is doomed to its own ignorance, but the effort is nonetheless commendable. I don't know enough to discourage you from the quest, so I give you my best in discovering knowledge that will help all of us.

As for books, I strongly doubt any species other than yours reads books by human authors. Humans have yet to demonstrate to us in any substantial way their value. I recognize that some of you make noble efforts at saving some of us from extinction. However, that likely wouldn't be necessary had not your species imperiled us by your historic disregard for nature.

We seem to have little to learn from your species, at least insofar as you have evolved. However, the inverse may be valid, as *jambbal's* fables aspire, in that you may learn much from the rest of us. We can exemplify for you many elements of survival. We can demonstrate, if you care to observe, how to care for the sea and land and sky around all of us, how to raise your young, how to preserve resources and how to live within your means without greed.

For these reasons, I give credit to *jambbal* for trying. I wish him success while recognizing that his success is limited only by your failure.

Introduction

He lived mostly in the 20th century, but his age was timeless.

His parents were European, but his racial and ethnic roots were blended from all people.

His language was Italian and broken English, but his words transcended any single tongue.

His occupation was constructing new buildings of the world, but his mission was constructing bridges of understanding for the people of the world.

His tools were words, but as a man of few, he chose parables.

He believed in the message of ages, the message conveyed by the great messengers, the message of the Supreme Being.

He believed in the message of **J**esus, founder of Christianity, to love one another, be kind and forgiving to the lowest wretch or vilest sinner, and treat others as you would have them treat you.

He believed in the message of **A**braham, father of multitudes including the Arabic and Israeli tribes, who avowed one Supreme Being and our common ancestry.

He believed in the message of **M**uhammad, founder of Islam, who proclaimed the truth of prior prophets and extolled the virtue of peaceful submission and obedience to the Supreme Being.

He believed in the message of the **B**uddha, the enlightened one, founder of Buddhism, which teaches clarity and understanding of the universe through contemplation and awakening to the meaning of existence.

He believed in the message of **B**aha'u'llah, founder of the Baha'i faith, which embraces all faiths, all prophets, and the unification of humanity through universal peace.

He believed in the fables of **A**esop, whose complex moral lessons were simplified into short, easily understood stories about humans, animals and nature that still have meaning.

He believed in the message of *L*ao Tzu, the founder of Taoism, which encourages one to live life simply, intuitively, unforced and with love, ever mindful of opposing forces that combine to complete the whole of anything.

He believed in all these messengers, and all their messages, which he believed was really only one message from one Supreme Being.

And so, he decided to try to be another messenger for this place, this time, these people, and beyond. And he took the name *jambbal* to symbolize those before him and in whom he believed and regarded.

The Bee and the Forest Dwellers

For reasons beyond our understanding, the animals who dwelled in the forest gathered one day in the secluded clearing beyond the waterfall, above the brook, past the meadow.

"Our forest is dwindling," shrieked the hawk. "I have seen it from the sky as I ride the wind bursts and soar high above the canopy. Man is cutting down our trees, one at a time, every hour the sun shines. The border of our beloved forest is shrinking, and we must do something to save it!"

The animals of the forest all agreed they needed to choose a leader. They set about the task of considering who among them was best suited to preserve their homes, their forest, their very lives.

The hawk, still in the position of speaker in the center of the clearing, exclaimed: "I should be your leader, because it was I who first brought this grave problem to your attention. Otherwise, you would not have known the forest is dwindling. My far-reaching vision and my ability to rise above the problem make me the best choice to be leader."

The catamount suddenly sprung into the center of the clearing, scaring the hawk. Peering at everyone with glaring eyes, he snarled, "Man is crafty and wise. As you all know, I hunt by stealth and strength and, as your leader, I'll stop this foe."

The deer cautiously waited for the catamount to yield the floor, then boldly pranced into the center. "Man is too powerful and too numerous to fight. We must be alert to the danger and swift to escape it. I depend on those qualities to survive and, as your leader, I'll share them with all of you."

The tortoise ambled slowly into the center and warned: "We cannot depend on man to care about us nor can we depend on our forest to last forever. We must depend on ourselves for shelter and for food. Unlike the rest of you, I don't rent my home; I own it. I know about self-reliance and, as your leader, I'll help you achieve it."

Then the bee buzzed in and all around the center, speaking as loudly as he could, which was not very loud.

"Shhh," all the animals said to each other so everyone could hear, because everyone knew the bee who visited them on his daily rounds to keep the forest fertile.

"I don't have the leadership qualities some of you have," admitted the bee, "and I'm not a very good speaker, but I do know how to live in a community that cooperates for survival. I know how to do a job and sacrifice personal desires for the good of the hive. I know how to preserve the plants of the forest by carrying pollen from one to another. I know how important it is to listen to each other and to share what we have."

The animals of the forest voted and they chose the bee to lead them. As his first official act, the bee appointed the hawk, the catamount, the deer and the tortoise as his advisors.

jambbat's **message: A leader who cares about all can be humble, quiet and small.**

The Snail with a Broken Shell

For reasons beyond our understanding, one evening that introduced to the countryside a warm, starry summer's night, a snail was sobbing very loudly, at least as loudly as a snail can sob. You and I can't hear it, but other snails can, even though they are mostly deaf.

Indeed, one particular snail did hear those sobs and slowly glided over to where the sobbing snail was nearly hidden beneath a cabbage plant. It didn't matter that the sobbing snail was nearly hidden, because snails can't see too well anyway; they sniff and feel their way along the trails they blaze through the gardens and woods and fields of green.

The concerned snail stopped well short of the cabbage plant so as not to startle the sad snail who was having a difficult time already and probably wouldn't enjoy being startled by a stranger. In a soft snail voice, the visitor called out to the snail in distress: "Hello, friend. Can I be of some help?"

"Oh!" answered the young snail from beneath the cabbage. "I didn't know anyone was here."

The visitor edged a bit closer and asked, "Can I help you with whatever is making you sad?"

Upon hearing a kind voice with what seemed to be a sincere offer of assistance, the young snail slowly crawled out from beneath the cabbage plant to feel and sniff and meet the stranger.

"I am doomed," announced the young snail. "My beautiful, sculpted, colored shell is broken and cannot be repaired."

"Oh my," replied the visitor. "You must be very frightened."

"I am! I am!" said the snail. "Without my shell, I will whither and dry and be eaten by some enemy, just like the one who tried to eat me an hour ago."

"What happened?" inquired the visiting snail.

"I awoke from my daily sleep as the sun went down to begin foraging for food just like every evening," explained the young snail. "When I reached the cabbage patch, all of a sudden, I was lifted up into the mouth of a toad who began chomping down on my shell to break it so he could eat me."

"That's terrible," replied the visitor. "What did you do?"

"Well, as you may guess," continued the snail, "I couldn't do anything but make more gooey-glop slippety-slop."

"Excuse me?" inquired the visiting snail.

"You know, if indeed you are a snail, it's the sticky stuff we make to stay wet and repel enemies."

"Ah," replied the visitor. "I call it mucous-pukous, because of what it does to our enemies who would eat us."

"Ha ha," exclaimed the young one. "I like that!"

"Let me see your broken shell," asked the visitor.

The young snail crawled far enough toward the visitor for inspection, and the visitor said something that surprised the young snail more than anything it ever had heard before. "It is true, my friend, as you suspect, your shell is broken beyond repair, but you don't need it."

"What?" exclaimed the young snail. "All snails need shells to survive. Without shells, how would we stay wet when it's dry? How would we protect our flesh when an enemy wants to eat us? Where would we hide?"

"Come closer," invited the visitor. "Tell me what you feel about me."

The young snail complied and moved very close to the visitor. "My gosh!" exclaimed the snail. "You don't have any shell, not even a broken one! How do you survive?"

"My young friend," explained the visitor. "I am what people call a slug. It is a despicable word, because it conveys a very ugly image of a pest. I am a unique being and I work very hard every day to survive without any protective shell like yours. The secret to staying wet and fending off enemies is your gooey-glop slippety-slop, as you call it."

"What do you mean?" asked the young snail.

"Your mucous-pukous, as I call it, serves the same purpose as your shell did. You simply have to make more of it than you usually make, but that's easy if you don't have a shell to maintain. With no shell, all the food you eat is used to take care of your body without having to take care of a shell."

"But a shell is so pretty," replied the young snail.

"Yes, that's true," answered the slug, "Being pretty is nice, but unnecessary for you to survive. Looking good doesn't always mean living good."

Through the rest of that summer, the two gastropods, a snail and a slug, formed a friendship that lasted through many summer nights and days. The young snail grew into a wise old slug who realized that knowledge is more wondrous than beauty.

jambbat's message: **Discovery is just around every corner of the universe.**

The Antarctic Bird Who Couldn't Fly

For reasons beyond our understanding, an Antarctic petrel was sitting on her nest incubating another bird's egg. Her own egg had been stolen by a skua gull, a bigger, more aggressive bird than a petrel, and somehow the other bird's egg appeared in her nest, but resembled her own, so she went about her mothering as if nothing had happened.

She kept the egg warm day after day until the life inside began pecking its way out of the shell. Shortly, a female petrel chick emerged, or so it seemed.

Mama Petrel took adequate care of her baby, but she was not really happy. The baby wasn't quite like the other baby petrels in the flock. Her colors were not quite like a petrel's brown and white colors; her legs were short; her body was rather dumpy; and she made sounds unlike the usual petrel sounds. Petrels in the flock smirked and made fun of the little one.

Nevertheless, Mama Petrel accepted the baby as her own; so she cared for it and protected it. Over the next few months, she left the nest for a day at a time to fish for small squid and tiny shrimp-like creatures called krill, then returned to the nest to feed her baby. These ventures were very stressful for Mama Petrel, because there was danger in leaving her baby alone. But fate smiled kindly on her and she nurtured her baby successfully.

However, as the baby grew, her wings developed strangely for a petrel. They were short and rigid instead of long and graceful. Her neck and legs were quite short. The flock mocked her, and when her friends began their flying lessons, she was so clumsy, they teased her even more.

Privately, the petrel chick felt a strange uneasiness throughout her entire chick-life, as though the flock might attack her without cause or reason. She grew up feeling afraid and alone.

When she tried to express these feelings, her mother would try to reassure her. "Don't be so suspicious of others," she would warn. "They mean you no harm. You are silly to even think that a petrel would harm another petrel. Your friends are just teasing you as friends do."

"But Mama," she would ask, "why am I so different from my friends?"

"Oh shush," the mother petrel would scold. "Just be happy you are alive and learn your lessons so you will grow up to be a good petrel."

But no matter how hard the young petrel tried or how long she practiced, she still could not fly. Soon she was at an age when her peers began to fish on their own. They would fly into the sky to locate swarms of krill and squid swimming near the sea surface below, catch them, and then return to their nests when they had their fills. She could only watch from the shoreline.

Eventually, she ventured onto the ocean surface and found that she could swim by kicking with her feet and paddling with her wings. Thus, she too could find small squid and swarms of krill just beneath the surface of the sea and feed just like the other petrels, although not as much since they were able to fly for great distances on their fishing expeditions.

As the young petrel gained confidence, she realized that many more squid and swarms of krill and even many small fish were swimming well below the surface of the ocean. She asked her mother: "Mama, can I dive deep underwater to catch more food?"

Her mother answered quite sharply, "No! You are a petrel. It is dangerous for petrels to dive deep into the ocean. Petrels fish near the surface of the sea; and they fly! You must learn to fly. Then you can care for yourself."

Alas, the young petrel could not fly like her friends. She considered herself a failure as a petrel, the Antarctic bird who could not fly.

As the seasons passed, her time of adulthood arrived. Her feathers grew denser. Her black and white colors became more vivid. Her body filled out so that she became the largest bird in the flock. Her thoughts reached past her mother's teachings. She began testing some of her own ideas to see if they were really disastrous or if they might work, if they could make a better life.

She discovered that she could dive deeply into the sea. By using her wings and tucking her short neck into her shoulders, she could actually "fly" quite fast under the water, not over it like her peers. And she discovered that by diving for as long as seven minutes at a time, not only could she gather more krill and more squid than other petrels who surface-fished over great distances for extended periods, but even small fish, as well.

Not long after her discoveries, a strange male bird appeared. He greeted her through his white-banded eyes, his black posterior and white front gleaming in the sunlight, using sounds surprisingly familiar to her.

"You, my lady, are distinct among the Adélie Penguins that I have known. I have been watching you among all these petrels for some time. You truly are an individual, a unique, beautiful, and wise penguin."

"But I am not a penguin" she replied. "I am a petrel like my mother."

"Believe me, my dear," the male reassured, "you are an Adélie Penguin, like me, not a petrel."

"How do you know such a thing?" she beseeched him.

"I know it, because you are black on the back and white on the belly, like me. You are unable to fly in the air, but you soar in the water, like me. You fish not on the surface of the sea like a petrel, but like a deep-diving penguin, like me. You can do all that, but your mother couldn't have taught you, because she's a petrel; and that especially is what impresses me. You learned to be a penguin all by yourself without any help! And you did it in the midst of a flock of petrels who eat young penguins and their eggs. I would consider it an honor to be with someone as remarkable as you. I would like us to be mates forever."

And so they were.

jambbat's message: **Lessons of childhood can be replaced by lessons of adulthood.**

The Finicky Frog

For reasons beyond our understanding, a young bullfrog grew dissatisfied with his birth pond, and decided to seek a new home.

His friends tried to discourage him. "Why do you want to leave here?" they asked. "Our pond has everything you need, and all your friends are here, too."

"That's part of the problem," the bullfrog answered. "There are too many frogs in this pond. I can't jump from one lily pad to another without bumping into one of you. It's just too crowded for me."

And with that, the bullfrog leapt out of the pond, onto the shore, and began hopping toward a new home, chanting all the while:

> "I won't settle down until I have found
> a place I can call my own perfect pond."

By and by, the frog found himself on the shore of a large lake. He jumped into the water to see how it felt. After only a few minutes, he began feeling sick to his stomach, because the waves kept tossing him up and down, up and down, up and down. He swam back to shore and looked out across the lake water. "There is no end to these waves," he said. "This is not a perfect pond. I will keep searching."

And with that, the bullfrog continued hopping toward a new home, chanting all the while:

> "I won't settle down until I have found
> a place I can call my own perfect pond."

By and by, the frog came upon a marsh. He jumped into the water to see how it felt. After only a few minutes, he jumped out, because there were too many birds and snakes and furry animals. "I could have no privacy or comfort in such a place," he said. "This is not a perfect pond. I will keep searching."

And with that, the bullfrog continued hopping toward a new home, chanting all the while:

> "I won't settle down until I have found
> a place I can call my own perfect pond."

By and by, the frog came upon a stream. He jumped into the water to see how it felt. After only a few minutes, he realized the rather strong current had carried him a considerable distance downstream. "I could not rest in a place that keeps moving me around like this stream," he said. "This is not a perfect pond. I will keep searching."

However, the current began to slow down, so the frog floated with it until the stream emptied into a small, quiet pond. The pond water felt good to the frog. There appeared to be no other bullfrogs, just a few birds, snakes and furry animals, and the water was as still as glass so he could see the tiniest insect wink, hear a dragonfly sneeze, or spot a hawk soaring overhead.

He swam out a short distance from the shore, quite tired from his day's journey. He spread out his big hind legs and lay very still on the pond water beneath the setting sun, resting, and chanting:

> "Now I'll settle down, because I have found
> a place I can call my own perfect pond."

Suddenly, without any warning, an explosion rose from somewhere directly underneath the frog and burst onto the surface of the pond with a violent splash and crash. In less time than a gasp, the spot where the frog had been was marked by ripples of widening circles across the pond's surface until they all slowly and gently disappeared back into the stillness of the pond water, not a shimmer to be seen. Far below, a Northern pike enjoyed the rare delicacy of a bullfrog dinner.

jambbat's **message: Every pond has its ripples.**

The Scared Stream

For reasons beyond our understanding, a stream emerged into the world one day from beneath a ledge on a mountainside, and began life quite frightened. Unbeknown to the little stream from deep inside the mountain where streams begin, a raging thunderstorm had just appeared over the mountain and, as the little stream poked its headwater from under the ledge, the storm announced its arrival with a blinding flash of lightning and a deafening clap of thunder.

The stream thought, "This is a scary place. I want to go back inside the mountain," and tried to trickle back up the mountainside.

No matter how hard it tried, the little stream could not return from where it came, for as everyone knows, water cannot flow up, only down. So it closed its little stream eyes and continued its path down the mountainside, shimmering and shivering at every turn.

Within moments, another bolt of lightning struck a large tree and a blazing fire came crashing down right in the stream's path. The stream felt the intense heat of the fire and became aware that its water was turning to steam and disappearing into the smoky air.

Desperately seeking an escape, the stream found a hole in the ground, perhaps an old woodchuck den, and quickly ducked into it underneath the fire. After an hour or so of digging through dirt and roots and stones, the stream emerged once again, but this time, farther down the mountainside and well past the fire still raging uphill.

The stream thought, "This truly is a scary place. I don't like it!" Yet, unable to undo its emergence into the world, the stream resigned itself to living with the dangers all around it and carefully continued forging a path toward the meadow at the base of the mountain.

By the time it arrived in the meadow, the little stream was exhausted, barely flowing and very frightened. As it made its way across the flat ground of the meadow, the stream met another stream that had emerged recently and was forging its own path. That stream had emerged on the other side of the mountain, which was protected from the thunderstorm and was quite happy and carefree. It bubbled and babbled and splashed and smiled.

"Hello, friend," called out the happy stream. "Come over the rise and join me so we can have fun together on our way to the river and the ocean."

The scared stream didn't know what to say to this stranger who seemed unaware of the dangers of the world. So it hid behind a grove of willow trees and ducked into a gulley going in the opposite direction of the happy stream.

Continuing on its path, all alone, the stream flowed through a stretch of woods, which gave way to a broader path. The stream stretched out to fill its new wider banks, and grew in size. Much to its dismay, plants and fish began making their homes in the waters of the stream.

"These intruders are scary," the stream thought to itself. "They make noise. They clog my waters. They jostle me with jumps and rushes and chases. They tickle my surface and bump my bottom, and they don't even ask my permission to live with me. I don't like it!"

So the stream continued its path not knowing where it was headed, but hoping to find a place where it could be alone, quiet, safe and undisturbed by intruders, surprises or dangers.

Eventually, the stream flowed into a large flat area with numerous tree stumps sticking up from the ground. A snake slid alongside the stream and said "Hello."

Startled by the snake's voice, the stream reacted without thinking, and said "hello" right back.

"Are you thinking of moving here?" asked the snake.

"Oh, I don't know," answered the stream. "What is it like here?"

"It is very quiet," replied the snake. "This place used to be a busy apple orchard, that is, until the fire."

"You have fires here?" asked the stream with more than a little fear in its voice.

"Not any more," replied the snake. "There is nothing left to burn."

"Do you have water plants and fish here?" asked the stream.

"No," said the snake. "Just a few insects, and a few toads who eat the insects, and a few birds and snakes like me who eat the toads. That's all."

"So this is a pretty quiet place, eh," concluded the stream.

"That's right," confirmed the snake.

"Well then," decided the stream, "this where I will stop flowing and settle down." And it did, and the stream was alone, quiet, safe and undisturbed by intruders, surprises or dangers. Moreover, after only a few cycles of the seasons, algae had formed over much of the surface preventing any plants or fish or other growth from making a home in the waters of the stream.

However, after a few more cycles of the seasons, the sun had evaporated much of the waters of the stream into the air, and the ground had absorbed much of the waters of the stream into the earth. Soon, the waters of the stream disappeared completely, and the stream was no more.

jambbal's message: **Life without obstacles can become a stagnant pool.**

The Divot

For reasons beyond our understanding, one springtime afternoon on a large golf course in a large city, a rather large lady quite unintentionally created a rather small divot.

Before it was born, the divot was a quiet clump of grass in a large field of grasses on the golf course, called a fairway. It had been very happy to be part of the family of fairway grasses. The groundskeepers fed the fairway grasses and watered them and fertilized them and made sure they were trimmed regularly to stay healthy and strong.

As happens so often with unintentional births, the newborn divot thought: "I did not ask to be brought into the world." Also, as happens with most births, the divot was propelled into the world by an irrepressible force, in this case, a not-too-good golfer who swung her club clumsily and lofted the little clump of grass into the air far away from the fairway.

In an instant, the divot, which used to be a quiet clump of grass among the family of grasses on the fairway, was all by itself, noisily floating downstream on the creek that ran through the golf course. As it felt the water tugging and pulling at the dirt around its roots, the divot remembered one of the lessons of the fairway grasses: "Your roots must be grounded in Earth!"

As it floated further and further downstream, the divot frantically tightened its grip around every bit and piece of dirt still attached to its roots. The creek's current tugged and pulled, but the divot held firm. The creek's water tried to dissolve the dirt, but the divot held firm. The creek bottom's rocks tried to jar the dirt loose from the divot, but the divot held firm.

Just before dusk, the divot entered a narrow stretch where the creek wound sharply to the right. The divot leaned toward the left edge of the current and, eventually, veered off toward the left bank. It settled beside a pile of dirt that had accumulated near the creek bank. The divot grasped with its roots for a hold on the pile and when it was secured, it rested, for the day had been very challenging.

In the morning the divot looked around and thought, "Perhaps this is my new home. I had best plant my roots here." And so it did.

However, plants take time to establish their roots. The divot had hardly begun to root itself when it heard a low, loud rumbling sound. To see what new danger might be looming, it stuck its grass blades up as far as they could stretch, which was not very far.

Approaching the dirt pile with considerable speed was a huge, yellow metal machine with a very large mouth in front of it. Before the divot could duck underneath the earth to hide, the machine scooped up the entire dirt pile and dumped it into another large machine, which then carried it off to parts unknown.

The divot was frightened, because it didn't know where it was being taken, but it took comfort in the dirt still surrounding its roots. It remembered the lesson of the fairway grasses: "Your roots must be grounded in Earth!" The little divot dug into the dirt pile as far as it could and held firm.

After a long journey, or so it seemed, the large machine stopped moving. The air stopped rumbling. The machine's body shifted and the dirt pile and the divot spilled out onto the ground...somewhere.

The next morning the divot tried to look around, but it was covered by a huge mound of dirt and could not make its way to the surface. It heard sounds of machines, not unlike the large machine that had brought it to this new place. All day the machines rumbled and vibrated the Earth, and moved it around and pressed it down. Then, as night fell, all grew silent and stayed that way for a long time.

The divot was still quite frightened at not knowing where it was, what was happening or when the next surprise would occur. The only comfort it could muster was the fairway grass lesson to keep its roots grounded in Earth. So it concentrated on its roots, grabbing every bit of dirt within reach, seeking out food, water, minerals, whatever grass needs to survive. Meanwhile the grass blades of the divot continued doing what grass blades and, indeed, all plants do: reach up for the sun.

Day by day, drop by drop, inch by inch and granule by granule, the divot established its roots in the Earth and sent its blades toward the surface where the sun shone.

A few inches below the surface, the divot encountered a layer of very hard, black sticky stones that were held tightly together by some sort of glue. It thought, "I can never break through this barrier. It is too hard."

But the memory of its fairway grass family would not fade, and the divot again concentrated with more intensity on making sure its roots were grounded in Earth, and its blades were reaching for the sun.

By and by, one day in late summer, the first blade of the divot's grass broke through the surface and looked around. There were no other blades of grass to be seen. There was no fairway. There was no creek. There was no mound of dirt. There were no large machines.

There was just a sprawling field of the hard, black sticky stone with lots of children running around everywhere and wooden and metal structures here and there. Close by was a short metal pole that made water whenever a child would press a button on it. The water would spill over onto the ground and the divot would drink. The sun shined brightly across the field and warmed the divot's blades.

Even though it no longer had a family of fairway grasses, the divot's new family of playground children made it happy, especially when they laughed.

jambbat's **message: Wherever you are, nourish your roots to reach for the sky.**

The Caterpillar and the Fawn

For reasons beyond our understanding, a caterpillar and a fawn struck up a friendship. They were first attracted by their differences, and later, by their similarities.

"You are so large, Fawn" exclaimed the caterpillar.

"You are so tiny, Caterpillar" replied the fawn.

"You have such smooth, tan and beautifully spotted fur," said the caterpillar.

"And you have such a rugged, bright green hide," replied the fawn.

"You can leap and bound so quickly, with such grace," said the caterpillar.

"And you can move so deliberately, so thoughtfully," replied the fawn.

"We probably can learn much from each other," declared the caterpillar.

"And we probably can teach much to each other," replied the fawn.

Thus, they spent many hours together through the summer and forged an everlasting friendship, talking, sharing thoughts, observing their world together, discovering how much they had in common.

Then one day, as the weather turned cool, the caterpillar began doing something he had never done before. He began making thread and attaching it to the end of a branch. The fawn asked, "What are you doing now, Caterpillar?" The caterpillar answered, "I'm not sure, Fawn, but something inside of me is saying I must do it."

"It looks wonderful, Caterpillar. Let me know when you've finished," exclaimed the fawn.

"Okay" replied the caterpillar. "I'll let you know."

But the caterpillar didn't contact the fawn, because the last thread he spun enclosed him inside the tiny structure, which blended in with the branch, the tree bark and the other colors and textures of the forest. Even if he had tried to contact the fawn, the caterpillar wouldn't have been able to reach him, because the fawn's mother had already secluded them in their winter den to protect against the cold and the snow of winter.

Months passed, and spring arrived with sunshine, blossoms and birds just returned from their southern wintering quarters. The fawn emerged from his winter den full of energy and curiosity about the sounds and sights and smells of life in the forest. He frolicked in the flowers, splashed in the mud, and raced through the glen. Then, he remembered his friend, the caterpillar.

The fawn found his way back to the branch on which the caterpillar had built the thread pod. It looked like something built by a master craftsman, its threads glistening in the sun, its walls tightly sealed and firmly secured to the branch. The fawn wondered what had happened to his friend, Caterpillar, and worried that he would never see him again. The fawn thought to himself, "This is my friend's grave."

Then, one end of the pod began to unravel from inside. The fawn watched intently. Shortly, a small hole appeared, out of which began to emerge a new creature, one the fawn never had seen before. The small furry thing wriggled itself out of the thread structure, and rested on the overhanging branch.

"Hello. Where is my friend, Caterpillar?" asked the fawn.

"Please wait a moment. Allow me to open my eyes and dry my body," replied the creature. "I have just been born and I'm still learning about the world."

"But I want to know where my friend is. He built this pod, and promised he would let me know when it was finished."

Stretching his body as far as it would stretch, and then unfolding surprisingly large and brightly colored wings that resembled those of an angel, the creature declared, "I am Caterpillar, except I have changed into Moth, a Cecropia Moth, like my parents and their parents before them. It is the way of all caterpillars from my family."

"It's a miracle that you have changed from what you were to what you are!" cried the fawn. "You are so much more beautiful than you were as a caterpillar. Do you think I'll change, too?"

"Naturally, my friend" replied the moth, "but not as I have. When you were inside your mother waiting to be born, you were the same as I was when I was a caterpillar, except I was outside. You will change according to the way deer change."

The moth stretched his wings outward, and continued, "Even now, you are different from when I last saw you. Go to the pond and look at your reflection. You have lost your spots, and you have two bumps on your forehead where a magnificent rack of horns will grow and spread out much as my wings are spreading out now. Each of us grows according to our nature, but each of us thinks according to ourselves."

jambbat's message: **Man discovered evolution; God created it.**

The Man of the Forest

For reasons beyond our understanding, an orangutan was transported from a large university somewhere in academia to a large forest somewhere in Malaysia.

He had lived all his 25-year life at the university after a professor of psychology rescued him as an orphan in the Malaysian forest. Funded by the university's program, the professor and his colleagues nurtured him, taught him to play games, and instructed him to communicate in sign language and to calculate mathematical problems. They often would gather around him as he learned new tasks, and remark: "He is quite smart for an orangutan."

His upbringing at the university enabled him not only to eat at a dinner table with proper manners and to use a bathroom in a proper fashion, but to share with and depend on others, and to be part of a larger community, qualities not characteristic of orangutans who tend to be solitary.

Whatever aggressive tendencies he may have inherited from his orangutan parents had been transformed into intellectual pursuits and civilized activities. He even enjoyed going to the movies and eating jujubes. Except for his hairy exterior, his short but massive physique, and his prominent cheek flaps, the orangutan appeared to be more human than ape.

And therein lay his problem. When the university cut back funding for its psychology program and forced the professor to retire, no other university expressed interest in continuing the professor's work with the orangutan. No zoo was interested in acquiring a great ape at such an advanced age for an orangutan. Even Hollywood was unwilling to gamble on a mature adult male animal with no acting experience. The only alternative was to return him to the place from where he was rescued 25 years ago.

The orangutan's first night in the forest was most uncomfortable. The forest floor was hard compared to his mattress at the university. Even the brush pile he gathered didn't seem to help. Much to his embarrassment, he awoke to an audience of forest creatures who had gathered around him, and as soon as his bleary eyes opened, asked, "Why are you sleeping on the ground? Are you ill?"

"What do you mean?" he replied.

"You are an orangutan, aren't you?" one said.

"Yes, I am," he answered.

"Then why" the inquirer continued, "are you sleeping on the ground instead of up in a tree like all orangutans do? Are you ill?"

"No, thank you. I am quite well," he replied, and, as the creatures began to disperse, he added: "It's just that I'm not from around here." But no one stayed to continue the conversation.

Tired, lonely and now growing hungry, the orangutan looked up into the tall trees. Their tops extended above the canopy of leaves beyond his sight. He decided to climb a tree, happily discovering that it came somewhat easily to his powerful body despite his 25 years.

Halfway up the tree, he was startled by a long, loud bellow followed by a deep voice: "Who are you and what are you doing in my tree?"

He turned toward the voice to behold another male orangutan, clearly older than he. Gleefully, he greeted him in sign language: "I am happy to meet you."

The old male grunted and asked, "What is wrong with your fingers? Can't you control them?"

"I am using sign language to communicate with you," replied the orangutan using his voice.

"I don't know any sign language," the old male retorted, "but I do know how to get you out of my tree so I can go about my own business!"

The orangutan was taken aback by such rudeness, and said, "Okay, I will leave you and your tree alone, but can I ask you where the kitchen is? I'm hungry."

The old orangutan snapped back: "What is a kitchen? There is no such place in the forest. If you are hungry, you must find the food in the trees and sometimes on the forest floor."

"What kind of food is in trees?" the orangutan inquired.

Puzzled by such a question from a mature orangutan, the old male asked, "If you don't know what to eat, how have you survived all these years?"

"I have been served by others," the orangutan stated with more than a little sadness, and then added with much pride: "I have dined with professors and mathematicians. I have broken bread in the finest restaurants and never have had to wash a dish!"

"Hmm," pondered the old male. "You've lived among humans, eh? Well, now you are back home where orangutan means 'Man of the Forest'. You had best begin learning how to survive in it."

A month later, after desperately trying to learn the ways of the forest by using the mental prowess he had acquired at the university, the orangutan fell ill from lack of food and sleep and from the intolerable stress of being unprepared to adapt to an entirely new and strange environment. As he lay near death on the forest floor, the creatures gathered around him, and remarked: "He was quite stupid for an orangutan."

jambbat's message: **Woe to those who are disconnected from their nature.**

The Jealous Herd of Jerseys

For reasons beyond our understanding, a few Jersey cows in a small herd on a modest farm on the outskirts of a rural town grew jealous of the farmer and his wife.

"Look at them," the most envious cow complained to her friends as she turned her nose toward the two humans who were in the yard preparing for the day's chores. "They come and go as they please. They have machines to help them do their work. They have a luxurious home with lights and heat and clean floors and tantalizing smells coming out of every opening in the house."

"You're absolutely right, Dear," agreed one of her friends. "Just because they're human, they think they're better than us cows."

"And what's worse," added another, "is they don't share any of it with us, and after all we do for them..."

"Yes, my friends," continued the first cow. "Every day they attach their contraptions to us and take our milk for their own use. Then they prod us out into the fields, rain or shine, to nibble on grass and hay and that awful-tasting feed."

"Oh please don't remind me of that feed," moaned another cow. "I'm getting so sick of it, and it's probably loaded with unhealthy additives to make us produce more milk."

The cows all mooed in agreement.

"And then," the first cow lamented, "they prod us back to that dark, cold, dingy old barn that's full of creaks and drafts and mice and bats, and expect us to get a good night's rest. Girls, we can do better than this!"

Together the small circle of jealous Jerseys all mooed louder so their sentiments would spread to the rest of the herd.

"What is the problem?" asked one of the other cows.

The lead cow delivered an impassioned speech about the discontent and challenged the herd to join the circle. Every cow, but one, voiced displeasure with their lot in life on the farm.

The one dissenter, an old cow rescued by the farmer from a nearby farm that had gone bankrupt, asked to be heard. The jealous Jerseys, confident that the herd was united in agreement, allowed her to make a statement, but only a brief one since she was yet a stranger.

"You are all complaining that the farmer and his wife have a better life than you," she began. "Well, that may or may not be true, but it doesn't mean that life is unfair, because each of us has a different way to live and work and play, a human way and a cow way.

"The farm where I used to live," she continued, "didn't have many comforts, because the farmer wasn't doing too well. For many years, we had a rickety barn that listed so far toward the pond that we feared it would fall over. Our feed was old and dried out, and took a long time to chew and re-chew before we could finally digest it. And our fields in the hills were hard and rocky, which hurt our hooves and made it difficult to graze. Life was not easy for us, but we hardly complained, because we all knew the farmer was doing the best he could do as a human, and so we did our best as cows. Eventually, the farmer got sick and stopped working, and the farm shut down."

"Well, that doesn't make it any better for us here on this farm, does it?" argued the lead cow. "We don't have to put up with human failings when it prevents us from having a better life and enjoying some pleasures, some luxuries, and having some fun."

"Yes," replied the old cow, "but don't forget that we are cows, not humans. We have our place, they have theirs."

The leader of the jealous Jerseys raised her voice, and bellowed, "Well, old Cow, you seem happy to have found a better lot in life than what you had before moving here. Now we want the same: a better life than we have had so far. Let's go, Girls!"

With that, the lead cow broke toward the farmhouse with the one-track determination of a locomotive. Their emotions fired up, the rest of the herd followed her past the barn, through the gate and into the farmer's backyard.

With a nudge of her nose, the lead cow broke the latch on the back door of the farmhouse and entered the kitchen, the herd right behind her. The farmer's wife was astonished at this invasion of her home and ran out the front door to the porch where she furiously rang the dinner triangle to summon her husband, the farmer.

By the time he arrived from repairing fences at the back boundary of the farm, the damage already had been done. Unfamiliar with human houses, the cows had trouble moving about from room to room. Not every doorway was wide enough for them to pass through without scraping their hides. Tables and chairs were knocked over, as well as vases, appliances, family heirlooms and knick-knacks on them. Windows cracked, railings collapsed, walls buckled and floors heaved. The farmhouse was a mess.

Unused to confinement in such a small space, the cows, one-by-one, began to panic. As the hysteria spread to the entire herd, one of the cows barged through a back wall and escaped into the yard followed by all the rest. In a cloud of dust, they rumbled back to their barn huddling close together the entire night.

Not long afterward, the herd of jealous Jerseys was invited into the homes of various humans who lived in and around the town, but this time as steaks and roasts and hamburgers.

jambbat's **message: Invasion without moral fiber tears at the fabric of civilization.**

The Bear and the Beehive

For reasons beyond our understanding, on a bright and cool autumn afternoon, a bear and a bunch of bees were arguing rather loudly, at least as loudly as bees can argue. The bear had been foraging furiously for weeks in the woodland, because winter was coming and he needed to store up body heat by eating as much as he could before hibernating through the cold season.

The bear ate all the nuts he could find. He ate all the berries he could see. He ate all the roots he could dig up, and many of the grasses, too. He ate all the fish he could catch, and even some small hares and squirrels. Once he even followed the scent of a white-tailed deer that had been fatally wounded by a novice hunter who didn't know how to track it. The bear feasted for many days on the deer carcass, but still wasn't finished gorging himself for the winter, so he continued his forest feast.

The past few summers had been quite dry and not as many flowers and plants had grown during the warm seasons. Still the bear had more than enough to eat, so when he smelled honey, he regarded it as a wonderful dessert before retiring to his den for the winter.

He followed the scent for nearly a half-mile to a beehive in a hole high up the trunk of a large decaying oak tree. He climbed the trunk easily, as bears can, and paused at the doorway of the hive to savor the sweet smell of the honey he knew was inside. Then he started tearing open the doorway with his massive front claws, and that is when the argument with the bees began.

Upon hearing the buzzing and growling and unkind words intruding on the calm order of her home, the Queen bee emerged to try to make sense of the situation. She was not intimidated by the size of the bear, but was nevertheless cautious in her approach, because in the many years she had ruled the colony, she had learned of bears' fondness for honey, honeycombs and even the bees themselves. She would have to call upon all of her skills to protect the colony.

"Mr. Bear," the Queen called out amid the clamor and din. "Mr. Bear, please listen to me."

The bear looked past the throng of buzzing protestors, and spied the largest bee of them all, the Queen. "What do you want," he grunted.

"I wish to appeal to your sense of compassion and community," she replied.

"What?" the bear asked. "I don't know what compassion is and bears don't belong to any community in this woodland. We are loners, every bear for himself."

"Well, Mr. Bear," the Queen continued, "you are part of a larger community whether or not you realize it. The woodlands are home to you, and us, and the flowers, and the trees, and fish and butterflies and so many other creatures and growing things. We all are connected in some way, and depend on one another to survive. That makes us a community."

"So, what do you want?" repeated the bear.

"Please" beseeched the Queen, "spare our hive. All the beehives have been weakened by summer droughts and long, bitter winters. Like you, bees need food to keep warm through the winters. Because of the droughts, many hives have perished over the last few years. In fact, our hive is the last in the woodlands."

"Well, that's a sad story," said the bear almost sounding compassionate.

"I have a daughter," continued the Queen, "who is ready to assume her royal duties. Next spring I will swarm off with ten thousand of my subjects to form a new hive. My daughter, the new Queen, will stay here with the remaining ten thousand to sustain this hive, and so there will be two hives in the woodland."

"Well, that's a promising story," said the bear almost sounding like a member of the woodlands community. "But," he continued, "I really don't care how many hives are in the woods next year. You are here now, and I want honey now."

"But Mr. Bear," pleaded the Queen, "you don't need our honey now, because you have eaten so many other foods to sustain you through winter."

"Maybe I don't need it, but I want it."

"Think of your children," continued the Queen in what now seemed like futile attempts to save her colony. "If you eat our honey now, they will have no honey next year or the year after."

The bear answered: "My children will have to fend for themselves just as I have had to do. They will learn to get what you can now, and worry about tomorrow later."

With that the bear tore apart the hive, ate all the honey and the honeycombs and the bee larvae leaving nothing for the hive to salvage or move. The next summer, without bees to pollinate the flowers and plants, the woodlands began to wilt and shrink and die. All the creatures of the woodland either moved or perished. The woodland was barren, and the bear had to find a new home in a woodland far away.

jambbat's message: **When the greed of a few feeds off the need of many, eventually all will go hungry.**

The Beaver and the Otter Gang

For reasons beyond our understanding, on a bright autumn afternoon, a gang of three young, boisterous otters interrupted the work of a beaver. The beaver had been repairing a small break in a dam he had built seasons before. The otters had been on a romp across many miles and many ponds before spying the beaver.

"Hey, beaver," one of the otters shouted. "Want to play with us?"

Startled in the midst of very carefully placing a branch into the dam break, the beaver looked up to see who was calling him. "What do you mean by 'play'?" he asked the strangers.

Upon hearing such a foolish question, at least to an otter's ears, and upon seeing the beaver's two very large, protruding front teeth, the otters howled with laughter until all three slid down the bank into the pond where they dove and swam and pointed at the beaver and made fun of him.

The beaver took no offense, but was pleased the strangers were gone, at least for a while, or so it seemed. He returned to his chore and was nearly finished when the otters exploded onto the pond surface with a loud splash right underneath him.

"Hi again, Beaver!" they said. "Come on and play with us. Have some fun. Take a break. Don't be so serious. Live a little!"

"Please be careful, youngsters," the beaver pleaded. "I have worked very hard to build this dam and keep it strong."

"Beaver, Beaver, Great Achiever!" taunted the otters. "Do you think you're better than us just because you can build things?"

"No," replied the beaver. "I just don't play very much. I work most of the time and take care of my family."

"Don't act so superior, Beaver," the otters retorted. "We take care of our families, too, or at least we will when we are old enough to have families. Bet we can stay under water longer than you can, Beaver!"

The beaver wanted no part of a contest, and certainly did not wish to argue with anyone, if it could be avoided. "I am no better than you or anyone else," he said. "I just want to go about my own business and not bother anyone." With that, he submerged into the pond's depths and slowly swam away.

The otter gang reacted as though the beaver had challenged them. "Let's get him!" they shouted, and they dove after the beaver.

The otters, being much faster swimmers than beavers, quickly caught up with the beaver, and began nipping at his broad, flat tail. Since the beaver's tail was made of thick, tough hide, he hardly felt any discomfort from the otters' sharp teeth. However, his sense of security was disturbed, and he feared for the safety of his family, which lived in a lodge not far from the dam. He swam in wide circles eventually making his way to his lodge to protect his family from the marauding otters.

Unaware that a beaver can stay submerged for up to fifteen minutes, the otters had to come up for air after only five minutes. "That beaver!" they ranted. "He thinks he's better than us. Let's mess up his dam!"

And they swam to the dam and began grabbing branches and twigs. They tossed them here and there breaking apart the mud the beaver had carried on his chest to bind the branches and twigs together to form the dam. Soon the dam began to leak, and ever so slowly, the pond water flowed out.

Meanwhile, the beaver gathered his family and led them away to another stream where he could build another dam, create another pond, and take care of them.

Eventually, the otters came upon the beaver's abandoned lodge, and made it their home for the winter. The pond froze, but still had enough water beneath the ice to sustain fish for the otters to catch.

However, when spring came, the pond had lost so much water it was no longer a pond. The frogs, the muskrats, the deer and the many other creatures living in and around the pond all grieved: "Our pond is no more. Our life in this place has ended. We must seek a new place to live, because this place can no longer be our home."

The otters didn't know how to repair the dam, because they didn't have the skills of a beaver. Consequently, they, too, had to seek a new home elsewhere, and in a short time, the pond turned into a deserted mud hole.

jambbal's message: **Laud the laborers on whose backs society perches.**

The Hammerhead and the Humpback

For reasons beyond our understanding, somewhere off the coast in a southern ocean near a submerged reef, a young male hammerhead shark cautiously approached a huge humpback whale of many seasons and, with all the respect commanded by such a magnificent creature, asked: "Excuse me, Sir, but would you show me how to sing your song and dance your dance?"

The whale ignored the small voice, or so it seemed, as he arched his back, thrust his enormous fluked tail, and with surprising speed for such a massive body, catapulted himself through the surface of the ocean into the air above.

"Oh my," the hammerhead exclaimed never having seen a whale breach before. "He is sure to drown up there out of the water."

Seconds later, the water directly above the hammerhead exploded as the huge humpback returned to the ocean depths with a twist and a turn and a wink at his startled admirer.

"How do you do that, Whale?" asked the hammerhead.

"With a strong flip of my tail, young man" replied the humpback.

"How come you don't drown in the air? All the shark elders warn us that the world above the ocean is dangerous."

The humpback issued a small giggle, at least as small as a 50-ton humpback can giggle, so as not to offend the curious stranger. "Since you are too young to know such things, I will tell you whales breathe air. We need to visit the world above the ocean every so often."

The shark was interested in whales breathing air, but returned to his original question: "Can you teach me your dance and your song?"

"Why, young shark, do you want to do whale things instead of simply being the shark that you are?"

The hammerhead swam closer to the humpback who clearly had signaled his acceptance of continuing this odd conversation between two different species of the ocean.

"Well, Sir," the shark explained, "I have been watching you ever since you moved here from wherever you lived before. Your songs and dances make me feel different than I ever have. They make me feel…uh, special."

"What do you mean, young shark?"

The hammerhead moved even closer to the whale's ear for fear another shark would overhear their conversation. "I have been learning about shark life as I grow up here. There are some pretty great sharks here, strong, smart, fast, hard workers, expert hunters and very, very reliable, I mean, you can count on them to be sharks every minute of every day of every week of every month of…"

"Shark!" interrupted the humpback. "What are you trying to tell me?"

"Please forgive me, Sir," he apologized. "It's just that I've never felt this way before and I'm not sure what to do about it, except come to you, since it is your singing and dancing that is making me feel this way.

"I have been taught that what sharks do," he continued, "not only is crucial to the survival of our group, but also to help the ocean survive by keeping it clean and healthy. The motto we learn is: 'Sharks are lovers of labor, so labor becomes love.'

"But after watching and listening to you, I wonder if sharks aren't meant to do something more than just work and survive. I mean these feelings I get when you sing and dance…I don't know. They are so new to me. No shark I know has ever described such feelings."

"Well, young man," replied the humpback, "I can show you how to do a few songs and a dance or two, but remember, you are a shark, not a whale. You will have to make the songs and dances your own, not mine."

"I will, Sir. I will," answered the hammerhead with excitement in his voice.

Some months later, after the humpback had left the area for his summer migration to the cold water feeding grounds, the young hammerhead male made his way into the inner circle of female sharks to find a partner. Unlike any shark before, he approached the group by dancing and singing what he had been practicing by himself all winter long.

As he neared the center, a very large, dominant female hammerhead confronted him with her head forcefully shaking back and forth, left and right, as hammerheads do, warning him to back off from the inner circle. In a loud voice so all could hear, she scolded: "What kind of worker would you be, gyrating and muttering into our circle like this? Haven't you learned how to act like a proper shark? No one would ever choose you as a partner!"

The young hammerhead had no choice but to retreat to the outer edge of the circle in humiliation. Near the edge, he was joined by a small young female hammerhead who quietly swam alongside him. After a while she spoke in a soft voice: "Watching you dance and sing made me feel...uh, different...special...like I've never felt before. Will you sing and dance for me again?"

And he did for many, many seasons; and, eventually, so did she.

jambbat's message: **Labor keeps life on the level; art uplifts it.**

The Tree Elder

For reasons beyond our understanding, one crisp November morning, the trees in a particular part of the forest were talking quietly about the Tree Elder, because trees are not in the habit of talking loudly. Their topic for discussion was the upcoming birthday of the Tree Elder who first sprouted from a seed in an abandoned cornfield 150 winters ago. The Tree Elder was an Eastern white pine tree, and was the oldest tree in the forest. It stood 130 feet tall and the tip of its topmost whorls, which are the layers of branches a pine tree grows each year, overlooked the rest of the forest trees: the birches, the black walnuts, hemlocks and spruce, and the younger white pines, most of whom sprouted from seeds of the Tree Elder.

It was they who were talking about the Tree Elder's birthday, and telling stories of the Elder's life and the history of the forest that grew up around the Elder. Even the bushes and flowers and birds and furry creatures joined in the conversation, because all the forest respected and appreciated the quiet leadership and strong protection the Tree Elder provided these many years.

"I remember losing half my family in the big fire almost a hundred years ago," recalled a large pitch pine. "If it were not for the wind shield of the Tree Elder's whorls, I and my sisters and brothers would have perished as well."

"My great-great grandfather moved our family to the Elder's branches a long time ago," exclaimed a black squirrel. "We have stayed ever since, because it is safe, and the Elder provides us with abundant food and shelter during the hard winters."

A euonymus, also known as a burning bush, suggested, "Let's have a gala celebration for the Elder!"

One of the senior white pines replied, "Euonymus, while you display brilliant red leaves that dazzle everyone each autumn, you may have noticed that pines do not show off very much. We are given to standing tall, swaying gently with the winds, and making little noise about it. Truth be told, we are rather shy and when we are noticed, it actually makes us somewhat uncomfortable."

So the forest agreed to honor the Tree Elder without fanfare, just simple homage paid the most respected member of the forest community who had lived long enough to have seen small tribes of people grow into large villages, the wolves and lynx and eagles disappear, and the crystal clear air turn grayish and cloudy.

One morning during the week of the Elder's birthday shortly after the sun rose, a new sound was heard approaching the forest, a sound unlike any made by an animal or bird or thunder or rain. It was a horrifying sound that made birds fly off their branches, chipmunks scatter into their holes, and willows quiver in their leaves. Soon, yellow steel machines roared onto the apron of the forest and began pushing trees and bushes down onto the ground, and rolling over them. They were making a wide path into the center of the forest, and didn't stop until they reached the base of the Tree Elder just before the sun reached the top of its daily arc.

"What is happening?" asked the trees and the animals. "Why are these men destroying us?"

In a while, word arrived from the "tree line", which is how trees talk to one another across the land. It seems that humans from some large cities were competing with one another as to which city had the tallest official tree for the winter holiday humans celebrate each year. Not to be outdone by mere city officials, the leader of the entire nation ordered his workers to find a taller tree to serve as the official national tree for the holiday, and thus, the Tree Elder had been identified as the tree of choice.

By sunset, the Tree Elder had been felled with a frightening crash and was loaded onto a huge machine with wheels, which then rolled down the wide swath that had been carved out of the forest. The remaining trees all watched in stilled silence, because trees don't cry.

A few days later, the Tree Elder was set in place by many workers on the national lawn, and thousands of bright, colored lights and glittering strands of silver were hung from every whorl, bottom to top. The Tree Elder was very embarrassed and, as it felt its sap drying up and its needles browning, it suffered more humiliation as throngs of people stood around gawking at it, singing songs, and bringing gifts.

Trees, as you may have learned, are not given to gala celebrations.

After the holiday, the Tree Elder was taken to a lumber mill where its branches were chipped into mulch for the national gardens, and its trunk was sawed into wide planks for floors and panel sheets for walls in the national leader's new summer home. The rest of the Elder's wood was shipped to a factory where it was made into matchsticks, one of which found its way into the hands of a careless camper who, during the following summer, accidentally burned down 1,300 acres of old growth forest.

jambbat's message: **Generations to create; moments to destroy.**

The Boding Bacteria

For reasons beyond our understanding, all the species of living organisms, from the highest form to the lowest, gathered at the Annual Conference of Living Things to address survival of the planet. The event first began when Karner Blue Butterflies voiced concern that their habitat in the pine bush was being bulldozed away by human real estate developers. The Karners' plea was so eloquent and the fluttering of their blue wings so moving that many other species enduring similar fates joined the chorus and an organization formed.

The Annual Conferences in the early years were very passionate, hectic and quite loud. Every species with a concern about survival, which included nearly all, tried to impress the others with their importance and why they deserved special consideration, especially the predators like the big cats, the big fish, the big birds and the big bugs.

The smaller species depended on their massive numbers to be heard and their brilliant colors to be seen. The bees buzzed about quite noticeably, while the ants swarmed into the meeting and took up positions in every nook and cranny. Mice scampered up and down the aisles handing out fliers about their usefulness. Jungle frogs and tropical birds flashed their multicolored outer wear in front of everyone's eyes and hummingbirds stuck their bills into every drop of conversation they could.

All were concerned about survival, and all were given an opportunity to say something about it, that is, except the bacteria. The bacteria attended the conference each year, listened carefully to what everyone had to say, and repeatedly tried to offer some ideas, but for all intents and purposes, were ignored by the others.

"Your problems aren't like ours," the other species would say to the bacteria. "You only have one simple cell to worry about; we have many complex cells that perform many complicated functions. Besides, some of your relatives produce diseases that kill the rest of us, so we're not even sure you are trying to help."

The bacteria were indeed simple single-cell creatures unlike the others at the conference. But they continued to participate as best they could, because they knew they had unique knowledge to offer. As single cells, they had a single purpose every single moment of every single day of their lives: survival of the cell.

The multi-cell creatures could afford to lose cells that were not vital to their overall survival. They also had other concerns throughout their daily lives, like finding mates, bringing up children, finding food and shelter, controlling territory, and competing for positions of prominence in their communities.

The bacteria focused only on the few functions needed for their survival and, as a result, did them very well. Their simple structure enabled them to live most anywhere on the planet in any kind of environment, hot or cold, wet or dry, high or low, dark or light. It also made them very good at taking in food and getting rid of waste. To make other bacteria, one simply split in two, no mate needed.

The bacteria would say among themselves, "The other organisms might learn something from us, but they all seem to be too busy, too loud, and too self-important to listen."

Gradually, the humans began influencing the agenda of the conference to include more and more social events, as humans do with great fondness. Everyone knew that humans thought of themselves as the controlling species of the planet, and were more than a little suspicious of their motives. However, everyone agreed that humans had wonderful parties, so they allowed some leisure-time activities, a few at first, and since such a good time was had by all, many, many more as the years went on.

The bacteria were not interested in parties, and as the conference became more of a social event than a meeting, they stopped attending. The humans reassured the other species that the bacteria's absence was not critical, and in fact, humans were working on ways to eliminate bacteria altogether.

As the years passed, some species disappeared forever. Some died out from diseases, others from starvation, and yet others from not being able to change as the world changed.

Every species tried to learn how to resist the increasing poisons in the air. Every species tried to learn how to find new food and different homes to make up for the lost forests, less fresh water, polluted oceans and harshness of the climate. Every species was in trouble. Gradually, only the bacteria developed the necessary resistance to toxins and diseases, and continued to find adequate food and places to live. Eventually, only the bacteria survived and took control of the planet to begin evolving life anew.

jambbal's message: **Listen to the lowly and be humbled by their wisdom.**

The Wisdom of the Wapiti Cow

For reasons beyond our understanding, an elder wapiti cow ventured upon a small group of young cows gathered at the edge of a meadow.

"Good day, young ladies. What brings you here?"

"We are waiting to see who wins the fight," one of them replied looking toward the middle of the meadow where two young wapiti bulls were engaged in combat. "We will stay with the winner, because he will have proved that he can provide us with strong, healthy calves."

The elder wapiti asked, "Who is prevailing?"

"It is difficult to say," answered one of the cows. "They have been on their knees with their horns locked for at least two hours."

"Oh, that's not good," the elder wapiti sighed. "I have seen such a battle once before. The bulls could not disengage their horns."

"What happened to them?" inquired the cows.

"Sadly," the elder explained as she winced from the memory, "they were unable to defend themselves against the wolf pack, and both perished."

"Oh my," the cows said, "we had better seek a bull elsewhere." One by one, they began retreating to the edge of the meadow as the elder wapiti cow slowly made her way toward the two bulls. They were exhausted. Steamy breath shot out their flared nostrils and gaping mouths into the chilled autumn air. Their knees were scraped from efforts to free themselves of their head-to-head lock.

"Good day, young men," she said. "What brings you to this meadow?"

"I am defending my territory," replied one.

"I am reclaiming my territory," replied the other.

"It is not your meadow," argued the one. "I won it in a fair fight with your father two years ago. Now it is rightfully mine."

"And I," replied the other, "will win it back for my family who lived here for many generations. This place is part of our history, not yours."

"History moves on," said the one, "and so will you!"

At that, they both began pushing and pulling, tugging and twisting, snorting and exhorting in a most furious fashion. But nothing came of it; their intertwined antler racks rendered them helpless.

Waiting for them to cease hostilities, the elder wapiti cow informed them of the young cows' departure. "It appears neither of you will begin a new family, at least in this meadow, in this season." Then she began telling them a story of how the Great Wapiti Spirit created the first wapitis placing them in a lush meadow so they could thrive. The two bulls listened to the elder who knew of such things.

"As the wapiti family grew," she went on, "the Spirit created endless meadows and mountains and rivers so that the wapiti families would always have a place to thrive." The bulls grew quieter.

"The Spirit gave you magnificent racks of horns and impressive height and muscular frames so you could attract cows and form families." The bulls paid close attention to her words.

"The Spirit created rules for fighting so that no bull would have to get hurt. Your onrush toward each other and the crash of heads looks violent, but rarely causes injury. Certainly," the elder concluded, "the Great Wapiti Spirit did not intend for young bulls to become entangled in their own horns."

Suddenly, as a key turns a lock, the bulls' grip on one another released. They arose, looked at each other incredulously, then cautiously backed away, turned and bounded toward opposite ends of the meadow. Just before reaching the edge, they paused to look over their massive shoulders at each other, and realized that the elder cow was nowhere to be seen. At that, each looked up to the heavens and together bugled a loud and triumphant wapiti call before departing to seek new pastures.

jambbat's **message: Wisdom from the spirit is the key that unlocks universal peace.**

The Holy Dale

For reasons beyond our understanding, a small group of forest friends was contemplating a journey to seek a special place in the forest, a place of legend, a place about which their grandparents had spoken reverently, yet had never before been seen by anyone in the forest. They were having a conversation about searching for the Holy Dale.

For generations the Holy Dale had been lauded as a place where all would be welcome in the spirit of love and peace and forgiveness and tolerance. No one would be turned away. Even natural enemies could overcome inborn instincts in favor of free choices for a better life. Every forest creature dreamed of finding the Holy Dale someday.

The friends' conversation occurred one midsummer evening an hour before dusk at their regular creek-side get together for the joy of having an end-of-the-day drink in good company. They had been friends for some time and genuinely enjoyed each other, which was no small feat given their backgrounds.

The eldest of the foursome was the boar, wise beyond her years, but always ready for a hearty laugh or a deep-throated grunt, as appropriate to the situation. She assumed the leadership position in the group with ease and commanded respect of the others who appreciatively recognized her attributes.

Surprisingly, the wolf was the boar's closest confidante. Were it not for their friendship, the boar would have been a natural target of the otherwise predatory wolf. They had met in a thicket some years ago, quite by chance, each attempting to evade a human hunter. They bonded in mutual interest.

The heron was the tallest of the group, its only airborne member and the only one with feathers that demanded constant preening. She was indeed quite pleasing to behold and, to the others' amusement, seemed rather aware of it. The heron strutted rather than walked, held her head high unless she were fishing, and often seemed to be looking at her image in the water rather than stalking her prey. The heron was vain, but because she knew it, she could laugh at herself and have friends who could see her inner qualities, not just her outer beauty.

The rattlesnake was the most recent to join the quartet. The heron had caught the young rattler one morning and was about to flip it up into the air to gobble it down headfirst. The serpent quickly anchored its body around the heron's neck. In his small snake voice, he appealed to the heron's willingness to let go in favor of a truce.

The heron knew she was an excellent fisher and would not go hungry by skipping a snake snack. Opening her long bill, she let the rattlesnake slip out unharmed, but instead of slithering away, the snake remained at the heron's feet not even coiling up.

"Why don't you crawl away, Snake?" asked the heron.

The snake replied, "I sense your kindness and grace, dear Lady Bird, so I know I am in no danger. It is not my nature to flee from anyone who treats me so." It was that evening when the heron introduced the snake to the others at the creek. Thus, in keeping with its abiding acceptance of life in all its forms, the group's unlikely alliances expanded to include yet another.

Their creek-side conversations flowed from interesting to creative, from humorous to challenging, but always reaffirmed the bonds between each other. Any arguments were settled or, if settlement could not be achieved, abandoned. Testy emotions always melted into the affectionate warmth cherished by all. Arrogance, greed, hatred and manipulation had no place in the circle of four.

On the evening the search for the Holy Dale became the focus of attention, the group had been discussing the difference between information, knowledge and wisdom. The heron offered the initial definition: "An informed individual is one who has learned to acquire and remember facts." All agreed.

The wolf followed: "A knowledgeable individual has learned to use information to try to understand life." All agreed.

The boar concluded the discussion as she so often did: "It is a wise individual who has learned to combine knowledge with wonder and, from time to time, discovers secrets of life."

The words inspired the snake to propose, "Well, then, let us act wisely and discover the greatest secret of the forest. Let us search for the Holy Dale."

Excitedly, the wolf noted, "Water draws all creatures for survival, so if we follow the creek, eventually we will find the Dale."

The heron volunteered, "I can fly, so it will be my privilege to act as the scout for our quest. From a lofty perspective, one can see things that remain invisible to those nearby."

The snake cautioned, "The dale is a wide, low valley, quiet and isolated. It marks the passage of time much slower than we do, so we don't have to begin the search immediately. It is said the Holy Dale has been there for generations and will be there for many more."

The boar, in her infinite wisdom, ended the search before it even began with an observation that pleasantly stunned everyone: "My friends, we do not need a place beyond our creek to encounter all that is attributed to the Holy Dale. You see, we already have discovered precious secrets right here among us, not because of a place, but from a state of being. We have created that loving, peaceful, forgiving and tolerant state simply by being ourselves, by being here, by being together. So, let us now say 'good evening and pleasant dreams' and then meet here again tomorrow evening."

And so it was for the rest of their evenings together, including some new members with each passing year.

jambbat's message: Inclusion fosters friendship and peace; exclusion fosters enmity and conflict.

The Vixen and the Grouse

For reasons beyond our understanding, a vixen passing by a tall hedgerow during a hunt to feed her pups was interrupted by a voice from the top of the hedge.

"What do ambitious cabbage farmers do?" the voice called out in a rather shrill tone.

The vixen looked up to see who had annoyed her with such a silly question, and inquired, "Who speaks from inside the hedge?"

"It is I, Ruffed Grouse. See?" as the grouse peeked out from behind the leaves near the top of the hedge.

"Aha," replied the vixen. "Now I can see you, but I can't hear you so well from such a height. Could you come down closer to me?"

"Well, perhaps just a little closer," said the grouse. "I have a very funny joke to tell you, so I want you to be able to hear it, but I don't really know you or if I can trust you."

"Of course, you can trust me," replied the vixen, as she flashed a broad smile from one corner of her tooth-filled mouth to the other. "I am always in the mood for a good joke," and she smiled again.

The grouse determined that someone with such a ready smile and sense of humor deserved to hear the joke clearly and hopped down a few branches closer to the ground where the vixen patiently sat on her haunches, still smiling.

"So," continued the grouse. "What do ambitious cabbage farmers do?"

"Well, I don't know. What do they do?" asked the vixen.

"They do anything to get a-head," the grouse chortled.

The vixen laughed, too, even though she didn't think the joke was very funny, but she broadened her smile even more. "That was a really good joke, Grouse. Do you have any more to tell me?"

"I have lots of them," replied the grouse. "I'm known by my peers as the funniest grouse of them all."

"Well, then, I am honored to meet you," said the vixen in her most gracious voice, smiling her smile all the while.

"Please tell me another, but come a bit closer, because it is still hard to hear you from so high up on the hedge."

Emboldened by the vixen's enthusiasm and comforted by her winning smile, the grouse hopped down a few more branches closer to the ground, deciding which joke to tell next. However, before the grouse could utter a word, the vixen leapt into the hedgerow, grabbed the hapless fowl, and brought home a fine meal for her pups.

jambbat's **message: A smile full of tooth may be a snarl, in truth.**

The Peacock and the Blue Jay

For reasons beyond our understanding, a peacock flew into a meadow patrolled by a very loud, a very busy, and a very observant blue jay. The peacock's equally loud entrance, as well as his brilliantly colored feathers and proud strut, attracted the blue jay's attention and admiration.

"What magnificent tail feathers you have," exclaimed the jay.

"Actually, they are not tail feathers, but extensions of my back feathers. It is called my train," explained the peacock. "My tail feathers are these short ones behind the train. See?" as he turned around. "They support the train so I can open it up and display it like a fan."

"Well, your back feathers certainly look like tail feathers," said the jay. "You are so clever!"

"And listen to this," boasted the peacock, as he shook his train so that it sounded like a thousand leaves rustling in the wind."

"You are the most spectacular bird I have ever met!" exclaimed the jay.

"Why, thank you," replied the peacock. "I am pleased to be moving to your neighborhood."

"You're moving here?" inquired the blue jay, eager to be recognized as the host of the meadow.

"Yes," said the peacock. "I have grown to my adult stage of life, and it is time for me to find my own territory. This meadow looks like a very nice place to settle down."

"It is! It is!" the jay replied in his most welcoming voice. "There is a great variety of food here, many prime nesting spots, and many good neighbors."

"That's good," said the peacock. "I think I'll stay a while."

"I can't wait to tell all my friends," replied the blue jay, and he hastily flew off into the surrounding hills and woods.

During the next few weeks, the peacock made himself at home and the blue jay made himself a daily visitor. Everything the peacock did, the blue jay noticed, and complimented.

"Splendid!" the jay would remark whenever the peacock strutted across the meadow looking like a prince in colorful flowing robes.

"Stupendous!!" the jay would shriek flying from one branch to another whenever the peacock unfurled his train into an arc of green that seemed to hold a hundred blue-and-bronze-ringed eyes.

"Absolutely supreme!!!" the jay cheered when the peacock chased off a rival peacock seeking territory in the same meadow.

One day, the peacock spied some delectable frogs jumping in a pond across the Highway. "I think I would like to fly across the Highway for a banquet I don't often have the opportunity to enjoy," he declared to his friend, the blue jay. "I have heard stories of danger about the Highway. What do you think?"

"Hardly any of our neighbors would dare to think of crossing the dreaded Highway," replied the jay. "But you are very clever and very courageous, Peacock. If it's a banquet across the Highway you want, then that's what you should get!"

Thus, his confidence heightened by the advice and encouragement of his new friend, the peacock flew across the Highway where all manner of vehicles sped by without regard for the creatures who lived in the meadow and the hills and the woods. He gorged himself on frogs, which peacocks regard very highly on their menu.

On his return flight across the Highway, the peacock miscalculated his weight after eating so many frogs, and unfortunately, failed to fly fast enough or high enough to avoid a collision with a speeding silvery sports car. The impact damaged the peacock's tail feathers so that he was never again able to erect his train. As a result, he lost his place in the meadow to a rival with a plucky attitude and a fully displayed train.

jambbat's message: **Beware of advice from those who offer nothing but praise.**

The Terrier and the Tiger

For reasons beyond our understanding, a small dog and a large cat decided to reside together. The dog, a wire-haired terrier, was always busy doing something; the cat, a Bengal tiger, remained quiet much of each day.

The terrier reacted to every sound, every movement, every smell, by running from one end of the room to the other and back again, all the while barking incessantly. The tiger remained quiet, observing the day unfold.

The terrier told the tiger about all the events of the day in great detail, and how he felt about each one of them. The tiger listened patiently, politely, even though he wasn't interested in many of the terrier's tales. He seemed amused at the terrier's continuous monologue, while the terrier thought the tiger should talk more, and would tell him so, often.

Early one morning, the terrier was cleaning the house, the vacuum running, the washer splashing, the broom and dustpan clattering, and all the while barking at every turn. The tiger, however, was listening to something past the terrier's frenzy, something ominous outside. He slowly moved toward the window and, much to his alarm, espied the dreaded Animal Collector approaching the back door.

Softly, so as not to forewarn the Animal Collector, he informed the terrier of the impending danger, but the terrier went on and on about the chores, and breakfast, and the dust, and never heard what the tiger had to tell him.

The tiger tried to warn the terrier briefly two more times before he fled silently out the front entrance to freedom. The terrier never saw him leave. He just kept on and on and on.

Shortly, the terrier was snared by the Animal Collector and sold to a circus for a modest sum.

jambbat's **message: Too many words, a flood; too few, a drought.**

The Wayward Wolf

For reasons beyond our understanding, a young grey wolf grew up with bitterness that he didn't fit in with the rest of the wolf pack. Despite his best efforts, he always seemed to fall short of being accepted by the pack.

His father was an albino, a white wolf with pink eyes, and stood taller than most other wolves making him that much more noticeable. As is often the case with albinos, he acted strangely, at least for a wolf. Consequently, the pack shunned him. The young wolf was embarrassed by his albino father and blamed him for many of his own difficulties with the pack.

The young wolf's mother was a statuesque, self-assured she-wolf who was attracted to the albino male's unconventional appearance and his forceful personality. During a period of unrest in the wolf pack while one leader was being challenged by another, she mated with the albino male and gave birth to the young wolf, a uniquely handsome male pup whose personality combined many qualities of both parents.

According to wolf pack law, once a new alpha male was chosen, the young wolf's mother had to pledge her loyalty to the new leader, and thus, had to disavow her relationship to her pup. Thereafter, the young wolf had to fend for himself, and did so with a grudge on his broad shoulders. He blamed his mother for going with the pack's new leader instead of staying with his father.

As he grew into adolescence, the young wolf didn't behave like the others. He growled and howled too loudly, too often. He boldly pranced about the forest and the meadow in full view of everyone showing off his muscular physique, well-formed muzzle and full coat of multi-colored fur. Such vanity was appalling to wolves who are known for being shy.

The pack labeled the young wolf "abnormal" and did not trust him. They shunned him and excluded him from pack games and rituals and secrets. His bitterness grew and he blamed the pack for being prejudiced and stupid.

As time passed, he developed into a strong, handsome wolf. He became cocky, and used his strength to challenge other males in the pack, usually intimidating them before an actual fight broke out. However, his boasts of superiority, stealth and stature eventually attracted a challenge from his cousin, an all-black, slightly older and larger wolf with a very short temper and no sense of humor who spent each day honing his hunting skills. The fight between the two ended quickly with the young wolf retreating as fast as his legs would carry him so he could lick a gaping wound across his jowl that eventually would heal into a prominent scar for life.

After his stunning defeat, the young male became an outcast of the pack, a lone wolf. He wandered the land, learning to rely on himself. Yet, each time he failed at something or bad luck visited him, he continued to blame others and grew more bitter.

On one occasion, he spied a small group of she-wolves at the edge of a meadow. As he had done so often in the pack, he pranced back and forth displaying his attributes in fine poses for the females, but instead attracted some hunters who fired off a few shots. The pellets missed him, but found the leg of one of the she-wolves, and condemned her to a three-legged existence for the rest of her days. He blamed the hunters for hurting the female, and the female herself for not getting out of the way fast enough.

From time to time, he would enter the territory of other wolf packs, but he was greeted with snarls and warnings to keep a distance. His failure to attract acceptance from other wolves bothered the young wolf more and more. He loped and moped through forest and glen and meadow and stream in a state of self-exile. He struggled to make it through each day. His search for food was reduced to catching small game, foraging the highways for roadside carrion, and occasionally snatching a hen or a baby lamb from human farmers. He blamed his parents, the pack, the world for his dismal fate.

As winter took hold, the wolf faced starvation. Not being a member of a pack, he could not enjoy the benefit of group hunts for large game, like elk or bison, the usual prey of wolves. He trudged through the gathering snow with increased difficulty until he was near exhaustion.

Then, as his strength was nearly depleted, he happened upon a large elder deer who had been wedged into a snow bank for quite some time, and was nearing his final hours. The wolf loomed over the deer and bared his teeth.

"Greetings, my friend," uttered the deer in a faint voice.

The young wolf looked quizzically at the old deer, and replied, "You call me a friend as I am about to devour you to save myself."

The old deer looked up at the gaunt, desperate wolf. "You are the future, my young friend. I am the past. You have the right and the responsibility to carry on. My time is over, my work finished. I only ask that you end my life mercifully and continue the tradition of the forest creatures to make things better for all. To do that, you must learn to forgive stupidity, ignore rudeness, and turn meanness into understanding."

The wolf interrupted his attack, and asked, "Why do you care about me?"

In a perfectly calm and gentle voice, the elder buck answered, "Because I am at peace with my life, and I am ready to pass on to the next, wherever that is. You, however, must stay here and seek your peace, and I hope you find it."

With that, the young wolf carried out the elder deer's request, and remained a few days to feast on the carcass and to gather his strength, all the while hearing the old deer's words over and over in his mind's ear.

One day, the wolf returned to his pack, older, wiser, no longer embittered. He issued a proper wolf challenge to the current alpha male, called on the strength of his parents and other ancestors, and emerged victorious as the new leader of the pack, and the pack flourished.

jambbat's message: **Blame and bitterness close doors; understanding and forgiveness open them.**

The Oak Tree and the Squirrels

For reasons beyond our understanding, a squirrel family was engaged in discussion about the oak tree they called home.

The oak tree provided the squirrels with protection from the storms and chills of that part of the world where they lived. It also gave shaded comfort during the sweltering hot sunshine of summers and yielded meaty acorns for the winter coffers of the squirrel family.

The littlest squirrel asked: "Who makes the tree? Who makes it grow? Who makes the leaves return each year? Who makes the acorns return each year after we eat them?"

The older sister replied: "It is the soil beneath us that nourishes the tree's roots."

The older brother disagreed, and said: "No, it is the rain that keeps the tree growing and renewing itself with special elements from the atmosphere."

The father squirrel said: "My children, listen to your father. It is the tree itself that possesses qualities of self-renewal to ensure its survival each year."

And the mother squirrel proffered: "You each may be right, but I believe it is the Tree Spirit that assures the life of the tree."

The squirrel family couldn't agree, so went about their squirrel affairs without further discussion.

One day, a storm visited the field of the oak tree and the squirrel family. It shook the soil drenching it with rain, then struck a bolt of intense lightning. The oak tree's branches ignited, and burst into flame engulfing the entire tree. The squirrels escaped in time and made their way toward a nearby oak tree that had escaped the storm's destruction.

The older sister said: "This didn't happen because of the soil, because the soil is still there with all its nutrients, so it couldn't have destroyed the tree."

The older brother said: "This didn't occur because of rain, because water stops fire."

The father said: "It couldn't be the tree's fault, because the tree is gone."

And the mother replied: "I don't understand. If there were a Tree Spirit, why didn't it save the tree?"

Then the littlest squirrel asked: "Who makes the lightning?" No one in the family had an answer.

jambbal's message: **To wonder is to ring the doorbell of God's house.**

The Adopted Squirrel

For reasons beyond our understanding, a red squirrel who was unable to have her own baby squirrels adopted a squirrel from a distant forest.

The baby was in dire need of a parent to give it nourishment and comfort and to teach it lessons of life, especially because it was a "hard-to-place" baby.

The reason it was "hard-to-place" centered on the baby squirrel's unusual appearance. Not only was the baby's fur grayish-brown, not red, like the other squirrels in the community, but it was smaller than the other babies.

However, the most distinguishing feature that set it apart from all the other squirrels was a flap of skin on each side of its body that extended outward from its wrists to its ankles. Whenever the baby squirrel tried to walk, the flaps would flop and fold, and at times, the baby would flip over, tripping on its own flap of skin.

The mother squirrel wasn't bothered about these things; all she cared about was having a baby to love and nurture and teach the lessons of life.

Nonetheless, as the baby squirrel grew up, the other squirrels would taunt it and call it names.

"You're a gray brown," some would tease, because of his fur color.

"Runt! Runt! Runt!" others chanted, because of his smaller size.

But it was "Flopping Squirrel" that stuck as his most embarrassing nickname throughout his childhood.

He looked to his mother for comfort and guidance each time he returned home from playing with the other squirrels. But his mother could only encourage him to be himself, to grow as he was intended and to be thankful for the blessings in his life.

He drew little comfort from her words and even less guidance, because he didn't understand what she meant. All he knew was that his friends scorned him and teased him and made him feel like he was a big mistake for ever having been born. Only his mother loved him.

So "Flopping Squirrel" tried very hard not to make mistakes in anything he did, and he carefully chose what he did to avoid failure.

One day, the group of squirrels was playing "Follow the Leader," a favorite game. They chose a leader who would challenge them with scampers and jumps and leaps and turns throughout the neighborhood. Whoever would miss a move would have to leave the game.

"Flopping Squirrel" usually would leave during the ground runs, because his skin flaps wouldn't allow him to maneuver the same way as the other red squirrels.

However, on this day, the leader chose an exceptionally challenging leap from the highest branch of the tallest tree in the forest to the branch of another tree quite a distance away.

The leader completed the leap with little room to spare. The next squirrel in line made it with a little less room to spare. By the time it was "Flopping Squirrel's" turn, which, as usual, was last, everyone had made the leap successfully, but a few, just barely. "Flopping Squirrel" teetered on the edge of the highest branch of the tallest tree in the forest. He knew the branch of the other tree was farther than he could leap. He stepped back.

The other squirrels began to taunt "Flopping Squirrel." They accused him of being scared, being different, weird. Then one called out, "You were adopted. Your real parents didn't want you. You were a mistake!"

That angered "Flopping Squirrel". He closed his eyes and said to himself, "I am not a mistake," then leaped out into the forest air with as much strength as his little body could muster. His leap fell short of the next branch and he began to plummet toward the hard ground below.

Instinctively, he stretched out all four of his legs. The air gathered under the flaps of skin, which billowed like a ship's sail. His fall became a glide. Excited, he twitched his tail, and his direction changed. He twitched it the other way, and once again his direction changed. He was steering!

He glided past the tree where his friends had landed. They were gaping at him with wide eyes and open mouths. He landed three trees past them; then looked back over his little shoulder. They were cheering for him and shouting "Flying Squirrel! Flying Squirrel!"

And he has been known by that name ever since.

jambbat's **message: Mistakes may be keys that open the door of discovery.**

The Weather Forecasters

For reasons beyond our understanding, a farmer was seeking advice from his farm animals. He had suffered three bad growing seasons due to unpredictable weather, and was desperate to make this next season fruitful.

"Two years ago," he explained to his trusted work horse, "I followed the forecasts of the farmers' books and magazines. I had been relying on them for a long while. Well, that year was a near disaster.

"So the next year," he continued, "I listened to the meteorologists, learned their lingo and read their predictions, all to no avail. That season was worse than the one before.

"So now, I'm thinking that animals are smarter than humans about these things. What can you tell me, my trusted horse, about this season's weather that will help me plant my crops successfully?"

The horse replied, "I can tell you the winter will be harsh if my fur grows very thick."

"Hmm," said the farmer. "Let me ask some of the others to see if they agree," and he walked to the cow barn.

"What can you tell me, cows, about this season's weather that will help me plant my crops successfully?"

"If the bull leads us to pasture," replied the eldest cow, "and we lie down instead of stand up, then stormy weather is on the way." The others mooed in agreement, and one added, "But if the bull follows us into the pasture, then it's anyone's guess what the weather will be."

"Hmm," said the farmer. "I'll ask some of the others to see what they think," and he ambled over to the pig sty.

"What can you tell me, pigs, about this season's weather that will help me plant my crops successfully?"

An old sow responded, "We all gather leaves and straw before a storm. Just keep your eyes on us."

"Hmm," sighed the farmer, and looked up at the rooster on the fence. "Can you tell me anything about the weather, Rooster?"

"If I go crowing to bed, I'll rise with a watery head," rhymed the rooster.

"Okay," reasoned the farmer. "None of you, except Horse, could tell me anything about the coming season, just today or tomorrow. Perhaps the creatures of the forest will know more, and he trudged off into the woodland beyond the cow pond.

The first creatures he saw were hornets busily constructing their nest. "What can you tell me, Hornets, about this season's weather that will help me plant my crops successfully?"

"You see where we are building our nest this year, Farmer?" they buzzed. "It is low in the tree, which means we are in for a harsh winter. If the winter were to be mild, then we would build high up in the treetop."

"Aha," replied the farmer. "Thank you. I'll see what some of the others have to say," and he ventured further into the forest.

A tiger moth flew past him and lit on a daisy petal. "What can you tell me about the weather, Moth?" he inquired.

"My babies, who you call 'woolly bear caterpillars', will tell you what kind of winter we are going to have with their body colors. A wide brown band means a mild winter; a narrow brown band between two wide black bands warns of a long, harsh winter."

"Well, that is most interesting," said the farmer. "Thank you very much," and he strolled on.

He discovered that many forest animals forecast harsh winters in different ways. Beavers build heavier lodges. Snowshoe hares grow furrier footpads. Bears sleep further back in their winter dens. Squirrels gather more nuts and do it earlier than usual. Not all the animals agreed about next season.

When he returned to his farmhouse near dusk, he lit a fire, brewed a pot of strong tea, ate a bowl of leftover pea soup, and pondered what he had learned from the various animals. There were so many different ways to predict weather, he couldn't decide who knew best. He listened to the evening news, read the newspaper, browsed through some agricultural journals and fell asleep in his chair.

The next morning, the farmer decided to prepare his next planting season using his own instincts and hoping for good fortune.

jambbat's **message:** **An expert prediction is no better than personal intuition.**

The Bull and the Bear

For reasons beyond our understanding, a bull and a bear were engaged in passionate discussion on their way to the valley market where all manner of business was conducted by the animals of the farms and forests.

Each had a single purpose of making money at the market, but each had a very different way of achieving that purpose. Each intended to buy and sell something that other animals needed, but each viewed the land and the world to which it belonged as differently as a smile is to a frown.

The bear lived alone. His mate and her cubs lived far away, as is the way of ursine families. He was responsible for no one other than himself. He roamed the terrain filling his belly from a large menu of forest foods and then slept all winter in his den.

As a self-made, independent individual, he knew all too well the ups and downs of life in the woods. He knew how fickle was the cycle of seasons and how unpredictable were the patterns of weather. He trusted in them very little relying mainly on his own prowess and judgment.

From his many years observing nature, he believed that events were more likely to turn out worse rather than better. He took precautions to guard against such disasters. The bear was a pessimist.

The bull lived in a large herd of many cows. He had many mates and calves, as is the way of bovine families. He felt responsible not only for himself, but for the entire herd and roamed the farm every day to make sure all was well with the cows and the calves, the pasture and the pond, the straw and the stream.

As a social animal, the bull had learned that there is safety in numbers and balance among friends. He knew that the herd could brace itself against cold winds and driving rains, warm itself from frigid temperatures by huddling close together, and sustain itself during hard times by sharing with each other.

From his many years observing nature, he believed that events were more likely to turn out better rather than worse. He made plans to benefit from good times. The bull was an optimist.

Not surprisingly, the conversation between the two centered on how best to make money at the market.

"This year will produce a bumper crop of clover," opined the bull. "So I'm going to the market to lease large fields of clover to sell to the herds all around the region at harvest time. I'll make a substantial profit."

The bear furled his brow and replied, "And, my foolish friend, what will you do when the crop rots in the ground and you have nothing to sell?"

"The crop will thrive," answered the bull. "I just know it will."

"Things don't always turn out the way you hope, Bull," cautioned the bear. "In bad times when prices go down and down, I make money by helping everyone realize that something they need may not be available in the future unless they depend on me to get it for them."

"How do you make money that way?" asked the bear.

"Well, this year I am dealing in honey, because you may have heard that there is a disease wasting away bee colonies across the pastures and fields. There may not be very much honey available by summer's end, so I am selling it now at a good price to make sure everyone has it later on when they need it."

The bull inquired, "But, Bear, how can you sell something you don't have?"

"On trust," replied the bear. "Everyone knows I can get honey pretty much anytime, anywhere. They will pay me a high price now to make sure they get honey later. When that time comes, I can get the honey much cheaper than I will charge everyone else today at the market."

"And what will you do if there is plenty of honey to go around by summer's end?"

"Trust me, Bull," assured the gloomy looking bear. "This Colony Collapse Disorder is real and will have a dire effect on us all for some time."

So each went to the market and conducted their business in their very different ways and then went home. By summer's end, the bee colony disaster was worse than even the bear had predicted. Not a single colony survived in the farms or fields or surrounding regions.

There was no honey immediately available for the bear to buy and distribute to everyone who had bought it earlier in the season. He was forced to buy very expensive honey from distant organic farms unaffected by the disease and, thus, were thriving with plenty of sweet honey. The bear made no money that season.

Nor did the bull make any money that season, because without bees, the clover in the fields he had leased wasn't pollinated and produced no more than one meager early harvest with very little to sell.

jambbat's **message: Pessimists need to see the sky, not just the clouds; optimists need to see the thorns, not just the roses.**

The Bald Eagle and the Golden Eagle

For reasons beyond our understanding, a young bald eagle and a young golden eagle were soaring on a wind draft high above a river that lumbered its way through a large woodland surrounded by a vast meadow.

Each glided effortlessly on wind currents without the single flap of a wing, flying in smaller circles until they were within speaking distance.

"Hello," the golden eagle called out.

"Who are you?" the bald eagle asked.

Somewhat surprised by his brash greeting, she replied "I am a golden eagle, and I have come here to hunt."

"What is a hunt?" the bald eagle continued his interrogation.

"A hunt is a search for food. And may I ask who you are and what you are doing here?"

Somewhat surprised by her retort, he answered, "I am a bald eagle, and I have come here to fish."

"What is to fish?" she inquired.

"To fish," he answered with a tone of arrogance, "is to find the food I eat from the river. What food do you eat when you hunt?"

"Golden eagles," she informed the young male, "eat all kinds of small animals, like rabbits, woodchucks, mice, squirrels, even some birds, like grouse and pheasants, and even snakes, too."

The bald eagle looked puzzled, and said, "I've seen those animals many times from up here, but I never thought of them as eagle food."

"Hee, hee," she giggled. "They are delicious, and usually, there are so many of them, an eagle never goes hungry, except in harsh winters and after forest fires and other disasters my parents have described to me. What do you eat, Bald Eagle?"

"I eat fish," he answered abruptly. "Bald eagles eat fish and lots of them all year round; and we never go hungry either, that is, except in droughts and floods and other disasters my parents have described to me. How do you catch your food, Golden Eagle?"

"Watch," she said, as she tucked her wings in close to her body, and dove toward the meadow. The bald eagle watched her swerve once, twice and then swoop down onto the ground. A few moments later, she returned to the sky to display her catch, a marmot. "Want to have dinner with me?" she invited the young bald eagle.

"Oh no, thanks," he answered a bit humbler than before the golden eagle's hunting demonstration. "My father has told me that bald eagles are not permitted to eat anything but fish from the waters. He said, according to a legend, it is the way it has been ever since a large fish saved the first bald eagle from starvation by swimming ashore and sacrificing itself if the eagle promised not to eat from the land, only from the water."

"Hmm," the golden eagle thought aloud. "Then how do you catch your food since eagles can't swim?" she asked.

"Ah, but we can if we have to," he replied. "Watch," as he tucked his wings in close to his body, and dove toward the river. The golden eagle watched him swoop down to the surface of the water and skim across it with blazing speed. Suddenly, with a ferocious splash, he grabbed a fish out of the river, and then settled onto the water where he floated for a while, and to her amazement, used his wings to paddle to the riverbank.

He began to feast on his catch, but not before looking skyward over his broad shoulder to catch the eye of the golden eagle. She already was gliding downward gently, slowly, and joined him on the riverbank. He looked up at her and said, "Want to have dinner with me?"

She replied, "Thank you. I would like that." And they each ate their own food, but accepted nibbles from the other's menu. The next day and every day thereafter, they hunted and fished and dined together, and they and their families never went hungry again.

jambbal's **message: Diversity feeds the banquet at God's table.**

The Wandering Albatross

For reasons beyond our understanding, a 9-month old wandering albatross was feeling anxiety while his parents were on an unusually long trip at sea. For nearly a month he had been waiting for them to bring his dinner as they had been doing since he hatched. He wasn't sure what he was feeling, but he was learning about the difference between hunger and anxiety.

His spindle legs felt tingly and his wings stretched out every inch of their eight-foot span until they locked in place, which felt strangely comfortable. As the weeks passed, his mud and grass nest at the edge of the cliff overlooking the water had become too small, too messy, too boring. His hunger made him uncomfortable; his anxiety made him restless.

But it was the sea breezes constantly blowing past the young bird that occupied him throughout most of each day. They seemed to say, "Come with us. Trust us. We'll show you the world." He couldn't understand what it meant, at least not yet.

He was growing up in the path of his parents who spent much more time flying away than sitting in the nest, but it was scary. Each time he looked over the cliff edge at the water far below, he felt the anxiety even more than before. He was scared by other large, mean-looking birds as they flew past his nest, especially when his parents were away. One even tried to enter the nest to start a fight.

Sometimes the breezes scared him when they blew by with such force they pulled at the mud and grass around him as though the entire nest would be lifted up and flung into the sea.

At long last, he spied his parents high in the sky, effortlessly gliding toward the nest with nary a flutter of wings. "Ah," he thought. "Dinner!" He couldn't have known this would be his last dinner with them.

"Mom! Dad!" the young albatross shrieked, as only an albatross can shriek. "I missed you. I missed you a lot and I'm very hungry!"

The albatross parents looked at each other in a way only mates of more than 20 years look at each other. They had done what they were about to do many times before with other fledglings and would do it again many times after.

"We missed you, too, Little One," replied the mother albatross. "Well, not so little any more; but now, time for dinner so you can grow even bigger."

After an especially large meal, larger than he ever remembered, and a short nap, the father albatross awakened him.

"Young man," said the father, "your mother and I have something very important to tell you. It is about your future."

"Sure, Dad. What is it?"

"This will be the last time your mother and I bring you dinner."

"What?" the youngster blurted. "How will I eat if you don't feed me?"

The mother albatross looked away over the ocean. This was always the hardest part of raising her children to adulthood.

"From this day forward," continued the father, "you will learn to feed yourself. You will begin this afternoon by jumping off this cliff into the sea breezes trusting them to take you where you can find food."

As his father spoke, the young albatross recalled the sound of the breezes and what he thought they were saying. Hearing those same words from his father gave him a feeling of confidence. Yet, the prospect of actually doing it this afternoon helped him understand the anxiety he had been feeling. He wondered if growing up was a mixture of confidence and anxiety.

Then his mother spoke, adding another surprising part of the challenge of growing up. In a somber voice she said, "Once you leave here, my son, you will not return to this place for almost ten years. You will live in the sky on the breezes. You will glide for hundreds of miles by locking your wings. The wind will teach you where to fly; the sea will teach you where to feed. You will learn to sleep in the sky and eat on the water, but only briefly so the monsters from below don't catch you."

His father then told him a story that would help him throughout life. "There are humans called sailors who float in boats. They will become your friends, because you are from them."

"What do you mean, Dad?" asked the fledgling.

"It is said among albatrosses," he explained, "that long ago, the spirit of the universe noticed that some humans were wasteful, because they did not care for their land or what was on it or in it."

"The spirit" he continued, "decided to teach those humans a lesson, so when they died, they returned as us, wandering albatrosses, without a real home other than the small nesting place on the edge of a cliff where we raise our young every few years, without any resting place other than the sky, and without a dinner table other than the sea. As sailors must depend on the wind to carry their boats from one place to another, so we learn to depend on the wind to travel around the oceans of the world. Follow the sailors and their boats, because what they do not keep for themselves will keep you fed.

"And, my son, remember this: our wandering teaches us to care about the world and everything on it and in it and that keeps the spirit of the universe alive."

jambbat's **message: Appreciate the space and time you are loaned in life by leaving your love in them.**

The Lamb, the Ram and the Ewe

For reasons beyond our understanding, the barnyard was unusually quiet. The rooster hadn't crowed all morning. The hogs hadn't grunted, not even when the farmer slung their swill over the fence. The mule hadn't brayed; the horse hadn't neighed. The bull didn't snort and the cows didn't moo. Not a single hen cackled nor was there even a peep from the field mice.

Only the chilled wind of late winter could be heard whipping across the frozen fields, rattling the hinges of the barn doors, whistling through the open cracks in the walls. And throughout the morning and many days to come, heartfelt sobs of the ewe punctuated the stillness of the barnyard. The only lamb-child of Mr. and Mrs. Sheep had died last night from a rare sheep illness. Everyone was shocked and saddened.

The animals gathered around the ram and the ewe to offer solace and support, but not too closely so as to give them room to grieve privately and to say goodbye to their little one. Barnyard animals know very well that the shock of losing a child is soon replaced by profound sadness and anger and bewilderment. Unanswered questions float around the fields and pens and stalls for years afterward, and nobody seems able to solve the mystery or soothe the pain.

"She probably was the most precious little lamb I have ever seen," exclaimed the old horse who all acknowledged as the farm elder. "We will miss her presence among us, but even more, we will miss the future she would have brought us."

Everyone nodded, some looking downward into the ground, some upward into the clouds, but no one could reply to the horse's words, which captured the feeling of the entire farm community.

Later that day after a particularly prolonged period of sorrowful wails from the ewe, the goat who was known for his testy attitude and straightforward quest for truth called out loud: "Why did you let this happen?" gazing skyward. "If you are indeed a Great Spirit that watches over us, how could you take away such a beautiful young life and leave two wonderful parents without a child to love anymore?"

The goat's words of anguished frustration touched many others in the barnyard, and the hens and cows and sows were moved to join the ewe in her inconsolable grief, and they all sobbed loud and long together.

The next day, fueled by the unrelenting sorrow around him and his own accumulated anger at such an inexplicable loss, the ram went into a rage when the farmer carted the body of the lamb away in his pickup truck. He butted anything in his path, even the bull who graciously took a step back to lessen the impact. Within ten minutes, the ram had spent himself and fell in a heap in front of the barn. The ewe knelt beside him and tried to comfort him.

As each day came to an end, the ram and the ewe struggled with letting go of wakefulness, as if doing so were death itself. Each night, exhaustion was their only usher into sleep. Even then, their dreams were disturbing images of their little lamb being overcome by various dangers and their inability to protect her. They woke frequently during the nights, still tired each morning. Their lives had turned from sweet to sour, without joy, without meaning, without purpose. Everyone was concerned about the ram and his ewe. They seemed to have stopped living.

Then one night, in the midst of an unusually deep sleep, the ewe had a dream quite different from her usual nightmares. In her dream, a very young lamb, not hers, appeared in a field of clouds and rainbows and waterfalls. The lamb was very beautiful, but she thought, not as beautiful as her own.

"I have a message for you, Ewe," said the little lamb. "Your lamb-child has become an angel of love and mercy. She is very happy, and cares for all the troubled souls that come here. She is a gifted helper of the Great Spirit who recognizes that she arrived already prepared for her role. It is you the Spirit wishes to thank for helping her realize her gifts so she could bring them here."

The ewe was startled by her dream, and just as she was wakening from it, the little lamb said, "Your lamb-child also asked me to make sure you continue giving your gifts to everyone in your life, because that is what helped her be who she is."

jambbat's message: Each life is a gift from God; each death begs to make sure we received it.

Lady Springbok and Mama Cheetah

For reasons beyond our understanding, Lady Springbok pronked nearly seven feet into the air, as springboks do, her back arched , her legs stiff, the white crest along her back gleaming in the morning sun, her head pointed downward toward the spot where she wanted to land: directly in the path of Mama Cheetah who was bearing down on a frantically fleeing lamb of the herd born four months ago.

The sudden appearance of Lady Springbok, seemingly from the sky, startled Mama Cheetah, and she came to a sudden halt. The cloud of dust stirred up by a cheetah suddenly stopping a 60 mile-an-hour chase was enormous. It took nearly a minute for the dust to settle. To Mama Cheetah's surprise, there stood Lady Springbok directly in front of her.

Instinctively, Mama Cheetah grabbed Lady Springbok by the neck, as cheetahs do, and put her to the ground. Yet, the mystery of why Lady Springbok would put herself in harm's way gave pause to Mama Cheetah's jaws, so they did not close as they normally would have.

"Why did you jump in front of me, Lady?" asked Mama Cheetah.

"Because you had chosen that particular lamb as your prey," answered the Lady.

"Why should that matter to you?" inquired the cheetah. "It's just another one of the huge herd."

Lady Springbok tried to clear her throat as best she could under the circumstances, and replied, "I know that lamb's mother and, due to one tragedy or another over the years, she has been unable to raise one of her own to adulthood. She is a good, caring ewe and is a wonderful mother," Lady continued. "She deserves the joy of seeing one of her lambs survive to maturity."

Upon hearing Lady Springbok's willingness to sacrifice herself for another member of the herd, every springbok within earshot began gathering closer to the scene, chanting softly, but in one voice, "Let her go. Let her go."

Mama Cheetah had never witnessed such herd behavior before. It seemed the herd's voice was coming from every corner of the veldt. It was very clear to Mama Cheetah that this springbok she was grasping was no ordinary springbok. She released her grip on Lady's throat, and took a step back. Gracefully, Lady sprung to her feet, but did not run.

"I have seen what a good mother you are," Lady said to Mama Cheetah. "You have two fine looking cubs in the brush over there, watching what you do and waiting for their meal. I also know that you, too, have suffered the pain of losing cubs to tragedy."

"You know that?" asked Mama.

"Yes, I do," said Lady. "I see many things on the veldt. Some gladden me; some sadden me, but I try to do what I can to keep the veldt safe for all of us so we can live together and raise our families and enjoy this life."

Mama Cheetah had never heard an animal speak this way. She thought springboks only had interest in grazing and running and jumping and standing around in large groups.

"You are right, Lady," said Mama Cheetah. "Life isn't easy for any of us."

"I know you have to feed yourself and your cubs," Lady continued. "I know it is natural for cheetahs to hunt springboks. I also know that one of our herd elders is nearing his end in a thicket about a mile away, if he hasn't already passed. His meat won't be as tender as a lamb's, but it will feed you and your family for days, if you get there before the lions and the hyenas. I just ask that you be merciful with him."

Mama Cheetah thanked Lady Springbok, chirped to her two cubs to follow, and loped off in the direction of the thicket Lady described. On the way, Mama told her cubs about the remarkable springbok she just met, and about how important it is to respect all the animals of the veldt to keep it safe so all can live together and raise families and enjoy this life.

jambbal's message: **To love a few is to be blessed; to love all is to be holy.**

The Song of the Swan

For reasons beyond our understanding, a swan of 13 seasons fell gravely ill and, although she didn't know why, she accepted her fate with the grace of outstretched wings with which she had soared the skies and the dignity of a head held high as she had glided across the pond where she spent her summer years. For all her adult life she was full-bodied, broad-winged, supple, and white-feathered as fresh fallen snow. Now in the midst of her affliction, she was gaunt, shriveled, brittle, and graying. Her world had shrunk to a corner of the pond where the water was deep enough for her to float freely, yet shallow enough for her to feed without too much effort, although her illness left her little taste for food.

She spent most of each day trying to float on the pond water, eating what she could, but primarily because floating didn't hurt as much as standing or sitting. She spent most of each night trying to sleep, but really just napping, because her body aches kept waking her and her mind kept reviewing her years of life on the pond.

Her corner of the pond harbored a sizable stand of tall reeds that offered some solitude and privacy from the rest of the pond's inhabitants, but gave ready access to her family and friends who wished to visit with her and to share memories and messages.

Her best friend, the Loon, surfaced in front of her after a long underwater dive gently breaking the water so as not to disturb her. "How are you feeling, my friend?" the Loon inquired.

"Not so well, Loon. I'm a bit discouraged," she answered.

"Well, don't get too depressed, Swan," the Loon beseeched. "You are the one who taught me to hold my head high after surfacing from a dive," as she dove and swam many underwater circles around the Swan before emerging with a flourish, her head held as high as her long neck would stretch.

"Your body is in a dive now," the Loon reasoned, "and you will need to come out of it with your head held high, just as you taught me to do. Can I do anything for you meanwhile?"

"No," the Swan replied. "I think I am fine. Thank you, my friend."

Her children, young and old cygnets, glided before her with the grace of their species, nary making a wave, a grace taught them by their mother. They all looked to her for guidance at this time of crisis.

"Mother, you have been with us our entire lives, helping us, teaching us, caring for us, and giving us strength and confidence and hope. Now it is our turn. Can we do anything to help you, to make you better, to feel more comfortable?" they asked.

"You all have been my pride and joy, each in your own way," she replied. "There is no more that a parent may expect from her children. You already have given me more than I expected, and now must pass those gifts on to all those you encounter in your lives. All of you are in my heart and there is nothing more I need at this point in my life. I believe I am fine, thank you. Now it is time for you to get on with your lives."

Her neighbor, the Snow Goose, waddled in quietly, and said, "I am so sorry to hear of your illness, Swan. I will do anything I can to help you through this difficult time, just like you helped me when I was sick and couldn't care for my own children. You simply took them in for however long it took me to get better, and then asked for nothing in return. You are a special neighbor. What do you need now that I might give you?"

"Thank you for your kindness, Goose," she answered. "I am fine right now. I am just tired and need to rest."

And so it was that multitudes recalled the Swan's generosity, her caring nature and her empathy with others. Yet, in her moments of solitude, she wondered if she had done enough, so she prayed to God. "Is there anything I must do here before I leave?"

And in time, God replied, "No. You are fine." And she was.

jambbat's message: **To sing with the heartbeats of others is to join the chorus of eternal life.**

The Source

For reasons beyond our understanding, at least as far as our understanding takes us today, life began at some time in some place. No one yet knows with certainty where or when or how it began or who or what began it. Those questions may be as old as the first life form able to ask questions.

One morning in her 14th year, a girl named Kamyyar was standing alone under a grapevine in the backyard of her grandpa's house. Her relatives and neighbors were all inside mourning the death of the old man. She did not want them to see her smiling or to know that she felt an inexplicable happiness for fear they would chastise her for being disrespectful. She herself couldn't understand her own joy in the midst of losing her beloved grandpa, but she was very sure that she could feel him with her and that he was smiling, too.

Kamyyar was born to loving parents, but soon afterward, her father died unexpectedly. Her mother despaired and sunk into a dark abyss of resentful obligation at having to live the rest of her life without her mate and having to raise her family all by herself. She became a creature of shoulds and shouldn'ts, dos and don'ts, have tos, not want tos. She went to work to make ends meet and forgot how to relax, how to play, how to enjoy life and the people in it. In a real sense, Kamyyar lost both of her parents.

Thankfully, Kamyyar's paternal grandfather lived next door and rescued her childhood by quietly assuming the role of a surrogate father. He literally took her under his massive, muscular arms providing her the gentle touch of a loving family member and the unconditional protection of a formidable bodyguard. He commanded considerable respect throughout the neighborhood, which was extended to Kamyyar by association.

By the time she was barely five years old, the old man introduced Kamyyar to his own homemade wine processed from the fruit of the grapevine in his backyard. Hand-in-hand, he would escort her to the basement, so no one would know he was giving wine to a child, and sit her beside him on an ornately carved rosewood settee with velvet upholstery. In her own special pewter drinking vessel, he would pour a few sips of the deep red wine and together they would talk for hours on end about the world, people, nature, life.

These private times with her father's father taught Kamyyar the joy of thinking and dreaming and wondering. During the decade of tête à têtes at their basement bar, the topic she most pursued was the source of life. "How did we all get here, Grandpa? Where did we come from? What was the first life like? How did it become us?"

The wise old man would claim ignorance, but always posed another question for her to ponder. Although she entered adulthood without the physical presence of her cherished mentor, she carried his lessons close to her throughout her life. When he died, she became acutely aware that she was wondering much more about where he came from than where he had gone. He had instilled in her respect for the lineage of one's roots and made her proud to be of his. She vowed to spend her own life on a journey of discovery in honor of her grandpa and with a mission to try to follow the lines of life back to their source.

To better understand life in all its forms, Kamyyar first went to a small mountainous island in the ocean to learn silence. Once she had mastered it, she was able to communicate with the mountain. Much to her surprise, the quiet mountain told her, "I came from an undersea volcano. I was born with a big bang!"

Next, she studied the amoeba to learn simplicity. Once she had mastered it, the amoeba told her, "I came from myself. I inhaled deeply, then held it until I nearly exploded and, suddenly split in two. My birth was breathtaking!"

She studied trees to learn of fortuity. She watched as they released their seeds to the wind only to lose track of them forever. A tree confided to her, "I was born quite by chance."

She learned about patterns from spiders, parenting from possums, survival instincts from sea turtles, perseverance from monarch butterflies, and when she studied salmon to learn about struggling to survive, a salmon told her, "I fight my way back to where I was born so I can give birth to new life and, not unlike your father, soon afterward I die."

Thus, she studied life in its many forms and continued searching for its source. When Kamyyar died, she went to that eternal place of souls where all gather into a collective unity of life.

As she entered, she caught a glimpse of an old man off in the distance sitting alone on an ornately carved rosewood settee with velvet upholstery. She was not surprised that it was her grandpa. She approached him with the same smile as when he had died nearly a lifetime ago.

"You are here, with me again," she uttered as they embraced, "and I am so happy to see you."

"As am I, my dear Kamyyar. Tell me of your quest for the source of life."

"I did not find it," she answered meekly, her eyes lowered.

"Are you sure?" he asked.

"Yes, I am, because my life has ended. Now I am here and I have yet to find the answer."

"Well," the old man posited, "you may have discovered the source without realizing it. Here, have a cup of wine," as he poured more than a childhood sip from a jug on the floor next to his seat. He turned to face her on the settee and gently touched her shoulder. "Life's journey took you from here right back to here rather than from here to there."

She rested the cup on her knee, squinted her eyes fixing them into a stare. She flashed back to all the lessons she had learned through life and reviewed them in light of what her grandpa had just taught her. Before long, her expression melted, her entire body relaxed, and her tears flowed. She exclaimed in a voice of triumph, "I understand, Grandpa! I understand!"

(I know this tale to be true, because Kamyyar was my granddaughter; I am *jambbal*)

jambbal's **message: As the source of life may also be its destination, we may learn more from circles than from lines.**

dedicated to Mary Kay
shown here with her Grandpa and Grandma Serafine
in 1943, just months after her father's passing

$19.95 U.S.